AF570797

Nostrums for Fashionable Entertainments

Nostrums for Fashionable Entertainments

Dining in Georgia, 1800–1850

Feay Shellman Coleman

TELFAIR ACADEMY OF ARTS AND SCIENCES, INCORPORATED
SAVANNAH, GEORGIA

This publication was made possible by an education grant from The National Society of The Colonial Dames of America in the State of Georgia in celebration of the Society's centennial.

On the front cover is a photograph of the Telfair Mansion dining room, which has been restored by generous gifts from the Demere family and friends in memory of Mr. and Mrs. Raymond McAllister Demere.

Library of Congress Cataloging-in-Publication Data
Coleman, Feay Shellman.
Nostrums for fashionable entertainments: dining in Georgia, 1800–1850/Feay Shellman Coleman.
p.
Includes bibliographical references.
ISBN 0-933075-00-6
1. Dining rooms—Georgia—Savannah—Catalogs. 2. Tableware—Georgia—Savannah—Catalogs. 3. Interior decoration—Georgia—Savannah—History—19th century. 4. Dinners and dining—Georgia—Savannah—History—19th century. 5. Telfair Academy of Arts and Sciences. I. Title.
NK2117.D5C65 1992 85-50257
747.7'6'0975872409034—dc20 CIP

All photographs of Telfair objects are by Daniel L. Grantham, Jr., of Graphic Communication, Savannah, Georgia, except #27 by Mary Carolyn Pindar.

The motif of the basket of fruit and flowers seen on the title page and elsewhere in this volume is an adaptation of the design of the central reserve of one of the marble mantels in the Telfair Mansion dining room. The design was drawn by Stacey Swigert.

Printed in the United States of America

Dedicated to the memory of
Wilma Mitchell Wierwill,
a tolerant and generous friend,
who endures as an inspiration
to both intellect and spirit

Contents

Foreword

Nostrums for Fashionable Entertainments is a publication with two closely related, yet distinct, purposes. First, this is the culmination of a project begun in the early 1980's to return the dining room of the Telfair Academy of Arts and Sciences, once the town house of the Telfair family, to its early nineteenth-century elegance. Fundamentally, *Nostrums* documents the superb objects from this museum's permanent collection related to dining. Initiated by the museum's director, Alexander V. J. Gaudieri, and encouraged by the board of trustees under the leadership of its president, Mrs. Dale C. Critz, this project would not have been possible without the initial vision of the late Mrs. Raymond McAllister Demere and the generosity of many members of the Demere family who so remembered and honored her and her husband. The second goal of this publication is to provide a vehicle for the dissemination of Feay Shellman Coleman's essay on dining practices in Georgia in the first half of the nineteenth century, when customs around food were regionally distinct. Our intention is to show how specific decorative arts objects relate to practices that were specific to the antebellum South and, in many instances, are no longer in use.

The Telfair Academy's publication of a portion of its permanent collection has been an effort carried out over several years. *Nostrums* follows *The Octagon Room* catalog of 1982 and precedes the substantial and comprehensive catalog of the paintings in this museum's permanent collection that is in progress. I want to acknowledge the persistence of Ms. Coleman, the author; Elizabeth Scott Shatto, who was on the Telfair staff from 1981 to 1991, including four years as curator-registrar; and of Pamela D. King, curator—all of whom have pursued this project to completion.

In addition to the Telfair staff, yet no less important, has been the dedication of support of this publication by The National Society of The Colonial Dames of America in the State of Georgia. Led by Mrs. F. Willson Daily, Mrs. Archie L. Morris, and Mrs. Robert V. Martin, Jr., the Colonial Dames in Georgia responded most positively to the proposal that the publication of this manuscript be supported with an education grant as a centenary project marking the Dames's good work in Georgia since 1893. I also wish to thank two Colonial Dames—Mrs. Pawling S. Steward, former president of this museum, who first proposed this collaboration, and Mrs. Leopold Adler II, a former museum trustee who personally supported this publication. Both ladies have strongly encouraged the publication of *Nostrums* and also the public dissemination of information on Telfair's important collection through the past decade. I am also grateful to the late Professor William Feay Shellman, Jr., who made a bequest to this institution that was applied by the trustees to this project. Given his life as a scholar and his interest in his niece's own devotion to scholarship, his generosity is a fitting bequest.

Gregory Allgire Smith
Director

Acknowledgments

It is a pleasure to review the entire course of the "dining room project" to recognize the support of friends, colleagues, and benefactors. A deep debt of gratitude is owed to the Demere family and friends, whose gifts in memory of Mr. and Mrs. Raymond McAllister Demere made the restoration of the dining room possible. The Henry Francis du Pont Winterthur Museum provided crucial assistance to research and manuscript preparation through the award of a Louise du Pont Crowninshield Fellowship. Finally, a major grant from The National Society of The Colonial Dames of America in the State of Georgia, with additional support from Mrs. Leopold Adler II and a bequest of William Feay Shellman, Jr., guaranteed the publication of this volume.

Alexander V. J. Gaudieri, director of the Telfair from 1977 until 1983, first envisioned the restored dining room and subsequently energized the project at every juncture. While steadfastly pursuing financial backing, he also succored and took great pride in the scholarship that underpins the restoration and this publication. Similarly, Gregory Allgire Smith has offered guidance since beginning his tenure as Telfair director in 1987.

All staff members at the Telfair and the Richardson-Owens-Thomas House have been unfailingly helpful. I am especially grateful to Dolly Tison and her successor, Olivia E. Alison, for their cheerful assistance. Elizabeth Scott Shatto contributed valued support consistently throughout the project. To her I am particularly indebted for assembling the collection records for the catalog entries. From organizing the photography to editing and fund raising, Pamela D. King offered just the right skill at many crucial junctures. The tireless research of the late Wilma Wierwill, our volunteer reference librarian, was both a mainstay and an inspiration to the project. Thanks also are due to Sheri Sterling, Rebecca R. L. Hayes, and Elizabeth A. Moore for their faithful transcription of copious notes and of the manuscript.

Research would have been difficult, if not impossible, without the kind assistance of the following institutions and individuals: Columbia University, Avery Architectural and Fine Arts Library; the Georgia Department of Archives and History; the Georgia Historical Society: Barbara Bennett, Tracy Bearden, and Anne Smith; the Henry Francis du Pont Winterthur Museum Library: Barbara Adams and Alleen Johnson; the Library of Congress; the late Terry Lowenthal; Frank G. Matero; the Metropolitan Museum of Art, Thomas B. Watson Library and the Print Study Room; the New-York Historical Society; the New York Public Library; Melanie and David Niemiec; Mrs. James J. Rorimer; the Savannah Public Library, Gamble Collection; Zachary N. Studenroth; the University of Georgia, Phinizy Spalding; the University of South Florida Library; and the University of Tampa, Martin A. Favata.

W. Carter Sims, Priscilla J. Brewer, James G. Jordan, Jr., Olivia E. Alison, and Harry H. DeLorme read the manuscript and offered thoughtful suggestions that helped me to refine the text. Frederic C. Beil's editorial expertise has been similarly beneficial.

And finally, for all the large and small kindnesses that are too easily taken for granted, I would like to express my heartfelt thanks to my family—especially to my husband, Joseph.

F. S. C.
JANUARY 1, 1992

Nostrums for Fashionable Entertainments

Introduction

From Mansion to Museum to Mansion:

THE RECREATION OF A HISTORIC INTERIOR

FIG. 1. Family group in a dining room, from Henry Moses, *Outlines of Grecian Costume . . .* (London, 1833). (Courtesy of the Metropolitan Museum of Art, Gift of Lincoln Kirstein, 1970.)

Introduction

From Mansion to Museum to Mansion: The Recreation of a Historic Interior

The purpose of the Telfair Academy is to preserve, exhibit, and interpret the works of art forming its collections; to preserve and interpret our two National Historic Landmarks—Telfair Academy and Owens-Thomas House; to enlighten and to educate all age groups through art-related programs and services; and to maintain a standard of the highest order throughout the museums.[1]

Nostrums for Fashionable Entertainments complements the restoration of the Telfair Mansion dining room (fig. 2), which is a permanent exhibition of the Telfair Academy. The room, no matter how carefully researched and installed, cannot be more than a visualization of the past, an exercise in preservation and exhibition. At best, this tableau piques the curious layman's questions: What was the methodology for making decisions about this restoration? What kinds of utensils were used for dining? How would one conduct a dinner in a room like the Telfair dining room? How was the food prepared and served? What kinds of menus were popular in nineteenth-century Georgia? By anticipating the visitor's questions, *Nostrums for Fashionable Entertainments* carries out the museum's mission to interpret as well as to preserve and exhibit.

The rich bequest of Mary Telfair—a mansion, furnishings, art, documents, and a library—mandated the essential focus of this study on Savannah's elite. Miss Telfair's legacy even inspired the title *Nostrums for Fashionable Entertainments*, which was borrowed from a small, handwritten volume, "Recipe Book for Puddings, etc."[2] Inscribed on the inside of the front cover is the name of Mary Telfair's mother: "Sarah G. Telfair." The book contains a handful of recipes and many blank pages. Toward the end of the volume are a few pages of girlish doodles undoubtedly penned

1. Bylaws of the Telfair Academy, April 26, 1988.

2. "Recipe for Puddings, etc." (Manuscript Collection 793, Georgia Historical Society).

Fig. 2. View of restored dining room.

by Mary Telfair or a sister. There are sketches of stylish ladies and a page that lists refreshments served at evening parties. Headed "Nostrums that are used at Fashionable Entertainments," this page (fig. 3) proposed the title.

The Telfair Academy occupies an unusual situation as an art museum residing in a historic house. Inherent to this juxtaposition are philosophical questions concerning the exhibition and interpretation of the building and decorative arts that have been thought and rethought over the decades. When the 1875 bequest of Mary Telfair established her

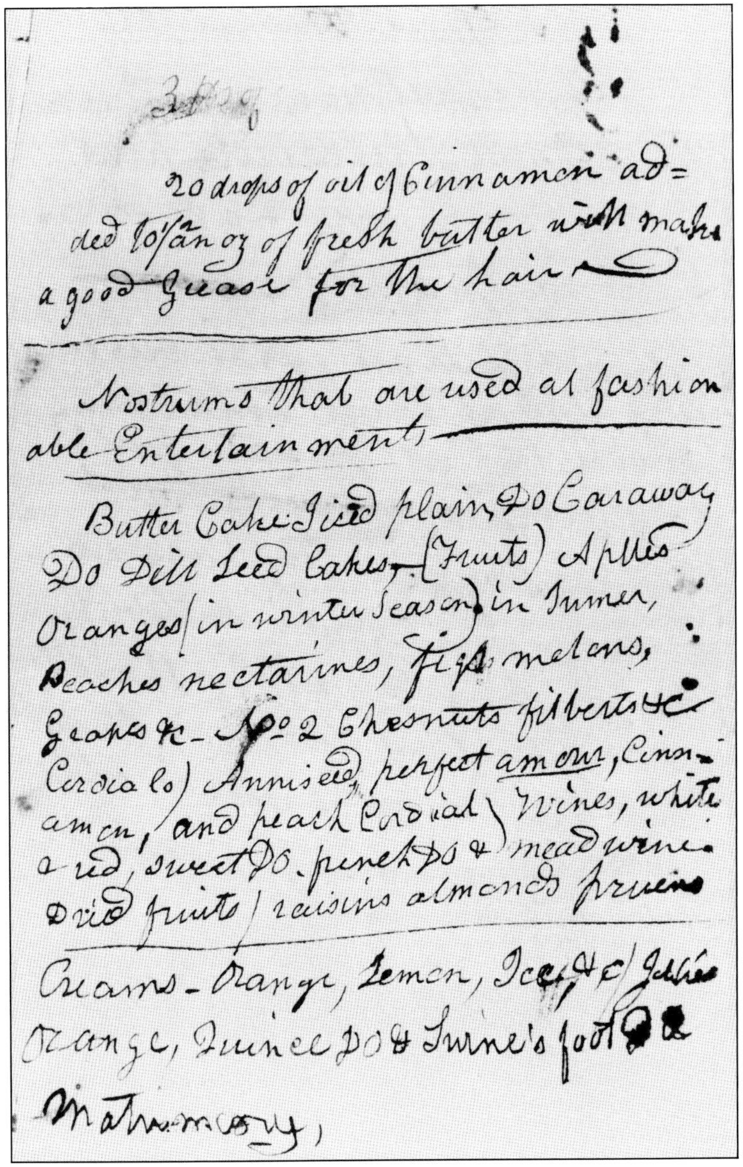

20 drops of oil of Cinnamon ad=
ded to 1/2 an oz of fresh butter will make
a good Grease for the hair

Nostrums that are used at fashion
able Entertainments

Butter Cake Iced plain, Do Caraway
Do Dill Seed Cakes, (Fruits) Apples
Oranges (in winter Season) in Summer,
Peaches nectarines, figs melons,
Grapes &c — No 2 Chesnuts filberts &c
Cordials) Anniseed, perfect amour, Cinn-
amon, and peach Cordial) Wines, white
& red, sweet Do. punch Do & mead wine
Dried fruits / raisins almonds prunes

Creams - Orange, Lemon, Ice &c / Jellies
Orange, Quince Do & Swine's foot &
Matrimony,

Fig. 3. Autograph manuscript, "Nostrums that are used at fashionable entertainments" (*ca.* 1820) by an anonymous member of the Telfair family; Telfair Family Papers, Manuscript Collection 793. (Courtesy of the Georgia Historical Society.)

family home as a museum of arts and sciences, the dwelling was already a vestige of Savannah's past. Mary Telfair's brother, Alexander Telfair, had erected the residence fifty-six years earlier during a moment of prosperity and optimism in Savannah.[3]

In the years after the War of 1812, and before the devastating financial panic, fire, and yellow fever epidemic of 1819–1820, Savannah flourished. Steam navigation of the Savannah River coupled with rising cotton prices brought unprecedented riches to the port city. No wonder Alexander Telfair and the prosperous merchants of his circle felt assured about building homes that would celebrate their wealth and high standing in the community.

The sixth child born to Edward and Sarah Gibbons Telfair, Alexander was a privileged son of wealthy and distinguished parents.[4] A Princeton education prepared him for a life in business, society, and public service. His coming of age as the patriarch of the Telfair family coincided almost exactly with the architect William Jay's arrival in Savannah during December of 1817.[5] Connected by marriage to two of Savannah's wealthy merchants, Jay stepped off the ship with one elegant home under construction and was to complete three more variations on the theme of the square plan villa in the next four years.

Jay's apprenticeship and early success in London, where Henry Holland, John Nash, and John Soane dominated the field, prepared him to reveal an astonishingly refined fluency in the Regency architectural vocabulary. His opportunity came with the commissions awarded by Richard Richardson, William Scarbrough, Archibald Stobo Bulloch, and Alexander Telfair. It took daring from both architect and clients to construct Grecian villas that in five short years changed the face of Savannah from a *retardadaire* Federal city into a harbinger of the Greek Revival.[6] Boldly situated on Trust lots designated for public buildings in General James Oglethorpe's 1733 plan for Savannah, three of Jay's four Savannah villas look out onto squares and recall the precious villas that Nash designed for Regent's Park, London.

By 1821 the boom days had passed. All of Jay's Savannah clients, except Telfair, lost their fortunes. In the early 1830's foreign visitors already viewed Jay's once stylish urban villas as moldering relics. At the time George Townsend Fox, a

3. For a biographical sketch of Alexander Telfair (1789–1832), see Feay Shellman, *The Octagon Room* (1982).

4. Edward Telfair left his native Scotland to seek his fortune in the New World. In time he settled in Savannah, married into the well-established Gibbons family, succeeded as a merchant, and entered politics, serving as a delegate to the Continental Congress and as governor of Georgia.

5. Alexander Telfair's last surviving brothers, Josiah and Thomas, died in 1817 and 1818 at the ages of thirty-three and thirty-two, respectively. Thomas, who served in Congress, was a rising star who eclipsed his brothers until his untimely death.

6. Born in 1792, William Jay grew up in Bath, England. Between 1809 and 1815 he served as an apprentice to the London surveyor D. R. Roper, who was involved with John Nash's development of Regent's Street and Park. Jay traveled to Savannah in 1817 and worked in both Savannah and Charleston until the early 1820's, when he returned to England. After receiving an appointment in 1836, he moved to Mauritius, where he died in 1837. Because of his relatively small output and early death, Jay's buildings, which dot the globe from England to the southeastern United States to Mauritius, are only beginning to receive the scholarly attention they deserve. See "Appendix II" for a list of Jay's designs and commissions documented to date.

merchant from Liverpool, visited Savannah in 1834, he noted in his personal journal:

> There are five or six very handsome and well built houses, which stand as monuments of the imprudence of their original builders who in a fit of excitement, when they thought they were rolling in riches erected them as more substantial monuments of their airy castles which have long since fallen to pieces. . . . One which cost $50,000 was sold lately for $10,000.[7]

Telfair family finances never faltered, but by 1832 death had claimed all the male children of Edward and Sarah Telfair. When Mary, the last of the nine children, died, she left her brother's villa, its contents, and an endowment to establish a museum as a memorial to the extinct Telfair family.

During the 1880's the first director, Carl Brandt, and the board of trustees engaged the New York architect Detlef Lienau to remodel and extend the original dwelling so that it could function as an art museum. At that time the dining room of the former mansion was designated to house the mementos of the Telfair family that had passed into the hands of the museum. These artifacts were exhibited in a "gallery" setting without regard for the original use of the room.

By the 1920's period rooms were familiar attractions at many museums, including the Telfair, where the Colonial Kitchens (fig. 4) opened in 1927. As time passed, furniture of the Telfair family, along with other items drawn from the museum's growing collection of decorative arts, began filtering piecemeal into the galleries that once had been the formal, public rooms of the Telfair family home (fig.5). With the reevaluation of the Octagon Room in 1981, the museum committed its resources to a program of restoring the architectural integrity of the three major, public rooms of the original Telfair family mansion.[8] The decision was taken in recognition of the achievement of the architect, William Jay, and to provide sympathetic exhibition space for the collection of nineteenth-century decorative arts.

In order to initiate the restoration of the dining room, the museum commissioned a team of archaeologists, preservationists, and historians to make a study. These experts used a combination of techniques to develop an understanding of how the dining room might have looked in 1819. First among the methods was a careful physical examination of the room itself. Contemporary documents—manuscripts, public records, publications—as well as visual materials—pattern books, prints, paintings, and trade cards—augmented evidence found in the fabric of the building. Bringing together data gleaned from these sources helped in making a plan for restoring and furnishing the room.

Found among the drawings of Detlef Lienau (1818–1887) in the Avery Library of Columbia University, an early floor plan (fig. 6) and cross section provided some keys to the original design. The plan illustrates clearly that Jay envisioned a room calculated to accommodate a large number of

7. George Townsend Fox, The American Journals, 1831–1868. (Joseph Downs Manuscript and Microfilm Collection, Henry Francis du Pont Winterthur Museum Library). Other visitors to Savannah, Tyrone Power (1834) and James Silk Buckingham (1839), also commented on the Jay mansions.

8. See Shellman, *The Octagon Room*.

FIG. 4 Kitchen, Telfair Academy, *ca.* 1930.

FIG. 5 Dining room, Telfair mansion, *ca.* 1930.

guests and convey the status of his client. Located behind the reception room and across the central hall from the drawing room, the dining room is at the rear of the "parlor floor." As they arrived, a servant showed guests into the drawing room before announcing dinner and opening the doors to the dining room. Spacious, even monumental, in dimensions, the room measures fifty feet six inches by twenty feet nine inches and is thirteen feet eleven inches high. The classically inspired decorative elements—deeply projecting and strongly profiled base, floor, and window moldings; plaster cornice ornament; two mantles; two chandeliers; and a rounded bay overlooking the garden—complemented the grand scale of the setting.

In Lienau's drawing the draftsman had inked in existing elements. On the other hand, anticipated changes and additions were penciled-in informally. While they are not Jay's drawings, they are the only early plans of any existing Jay building in Savannah. The plans did not answer every question concerning the restoration; yet taken with an examination of the fabric of the building, they imparted solutions to most dilemmas.

Lienau's drawing showed that the architect and museum director—respecting the essence of the original designer's concept for the room—had proceeded conservatively with their alterations of the building. Except a doorway to the central hall that was eliminated and a doorway to the new annex that was created, the plan of the room remained intact. Among the survivals of the Jay design were the base

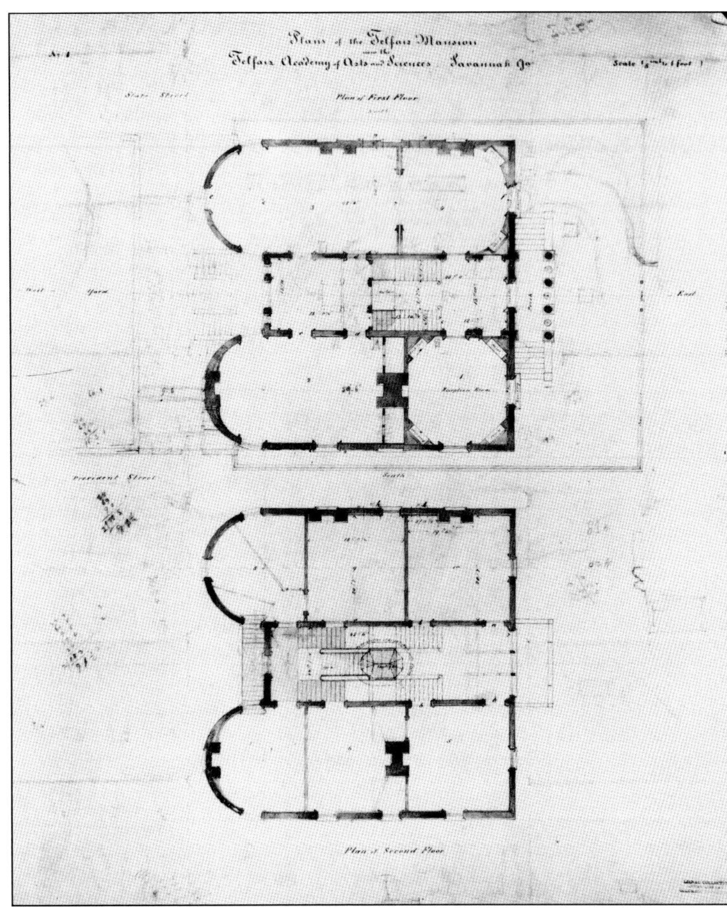

Fig. 6. Detlef Lienau, "Plans of the Telfair Mansion now the Telfair Academy of Arts and Sciences, Savannah, Ga." (*ca.* 1883). (Courtesy of the Avery Architectural and Fine Arts Library, Columbia University.)

moldings and door enframements, from which a molding profile was lifted to guide the millwork for the restored doorframe. Even though a thorough search of basements, attics, closets, and out-of-the-way places is apt to turn up original elements that were recycled rather than discarded, none of Jay's original doors was found. Careful sleuthing of the doorframes, however, yielded enough clues to recreate the doors. The paneling pattern, consisting of one elongated, recessed rectangle, is reflected in the existing side panels. Lock catches at the top center of the doorframe signaled that the opening had been fitted out with double doors. Plates in pattern books contemporaneous with the house confirm the taste for elongated vertical paneling schemes in double doors.[9] Door furniture had been discarded with the doors. However, period hardware—knobs and keepers—survived at the Richardson-Owens-Thomas House, also designed by Jay, and served as models for reproductions used in the Telfair dining room.

The cornice presented more difficulties. Physical examination showed that the empty plaster cove had once harbored an ornament. Careful scrutiny of the lip of the cove led to the discovery of disturbances in the surface of the plaster that indicated the original ornaments had been placed on seven and a half–inch centers. From this evidence it was possible to adapt a suitable cornice ornament from the Richardson-Owens-Thomas House.

To have most of the cornice was a great bit of luck. The case of the ceiling and walls was not so fortuitous. The original plaster ceiling, a victim of time, had been replaced, leaving no traces of the original appearance. As the physical

9. See Charles A. Busby, *A Collection of Designs for Modern Embellishments Suitable to Parlours, . . . Etc.* (1810), plate 12.

process of restoration began, the modern ceiling plaster required removal. The exposed lathe divulged fittings for anchors and abandoned gas jets for not one, but two, chandeliers. Since nothing remained of the original medallions, appropriate period examples were selected and reproduced. At this writing the whereabouts of the original chandeliers are unknown and substitutes have not been procured.

Fireplaces at each end of the room retain their original mantles. Since ships's manifests demonstrate that Jay imported from England products such as "Fifteen Cases and Two Bundles contg. Marble Chimney Pieces & Grates," it is unusual to find American mantles in the dining room.[10] The bold Regency exuberance of the base moldings contrasts pointedly with the Federal restraint of the mantles. Although classically inspired, the mantles embody the compartmentalized decoration of the Federal era. Each has a gray marble frieze interrupted by a central reserve carved with fruit- and flower-filled baskets and flanked by two smaller reserves directly above Ionic capitals raised on plain shafts. Perhaps the client's taste is the key to the anomaly.

Aside from the original mantles that remained in place, very little else of the wall treatment was undisturbed. In order to faithfully reproduce colors, paint chips taken from the woodwork and the plaster cornice were microanalyzed and matched to color swatches. On the other hand, the color of the walls had been lost with the original plaster, thus forcing researchers to consider what might have been rather than what was.

10. Entry of Merchandise, (May 18, 1819), Bureau of Customs, Savannah (National Archives).

Although paint histories survived in other Jay rooms and there are ample works on wall colors of choice for the period, researchers decided to broaden their perspective in considering the treatment of the walls. Immensely popular in the early nineteenth century, panoramic wallpapers and block-printed murals presented an option. In 1814 Joseph Dufour of Paris published one of the most dramatic and beautiful of these papers: "The Monuments of Paris." Notices in American newspapers indicate that Dufour distributed "The Monuments of Paris" widely, even as widely as Savannah because *The Savannah Republican* of January 11, 1817, printed the following: "*New Goods*—DUEL, GRESHAM & Co. have now Landing A few cases of very superb Paper Hangings, in sets representing hunting scenes, views of the Monuments of Paris, etc."[11] Likewise, there appeared on November 13, 1818, "Elegant Paper Hangings. Just received a variety of elegant French paper hangings, with splendid borders; also some very low priced."[12] Guided by these advertisements and the knowledge that scenic wallpapers with borders were often used in dining rooms, and that, indeed, "The Monuments of Paris" was featured in the "picture paper room" at Friendfield, a plantation near Georgetown, South Carolina, the decision was taken to install the French scenic wallpaper, "The Monuments of Paris," with a drapery swag border in the Telfair dining room.[13]

Semipermanent fixtures, such as floor and window treatments, complete the architectural setting for movable furnishings. The notation "Carpet and Rug in Dining Room"

11. *The Savannah Republican* (January 11, 1817).
12. Unidentified newspaper (November 13, 1818).
13. See William Rotch Ware, *The Georgian Period: . . .* (1923), plates 280–282.

in the 1833 estate inventory of Alexander Telfair provided a general indication that the room was probably fitted out with a wall-to-wall carpet and hearth rug.[14] "A Brusselles carpet" and "a rug to suit" found in the 1822 record of the sale of dining room furnishings from the Jay villa owned by Richard Richardson (now the Richardson-Owens-Thomas House) confirmed the suitability of such a floor treatment in the Telfair dining room.[15] Savannah merchants frequently advertised the arrival of "rolls [of] Brussel's carpeting" from England.[16] Likewise, the reproduction carpet and border selected for the Telfair dining room were woven at an English mill in thirty-six-inch wide strips and shipped to the United States in rolls. Then the strips were cut to the proper length, sewed together, and finished with a border.

Because window treatments did not appear in Alexander Telfair's estate inventory, the 1822 sales of Richard Richardson and of Archibald Bulloch, another Jay client, yielded the best clue to how Telfair might have outfitted his dining room. "Window curtains and ornaments" and "Gilt window cornishes" with "curtains to suit" embellished the Richardson and Bulloch dining rooms, respectively.[17] Once satisfied that the Telfair dining room would have had cornices and curtains, the archives of Gillow and Company, an English decorating firm, supplied a design to complement the classical disposition of the room.[18] The Gillow watercolor dictated the rich blue reproduction drapery fabric arranged with folds and flat pleats topped by rosettes. The window treatments are finished out with mull curtains held in place by stamped metal knobs reprising the rosette motif of the curtains.

Moving from the architectural to the cultural environment, *Nostrums for Fashionable Entertainments* is based on a parallel methodology of research and analysis. A curiosity about what a guest of the Telfairs might have experienced led the researcher to a diverse pool of authorities. For the curator, the first clues came from examining objects as disparate as the framework of a historic structure and the innards of a silver coffee pot. How a thing looks, works, and feels to the hand tells something of its maker and owner. Reports on archaeological investigations provided an even richer mix of materials from artifacts to the remains of table scraps. Analysis of paintings, prints, drawings, and even scribbles yielded visual guideposts to the epoch. Both newspaper advertisements and books on cooking, domestic management, and etiquette suggested theoretical benchmarks, while personal narratives from the period—diaries, letters, reminiscences, and travellers' accounts—told something of how theory was put into practice. Finally, legal records of deeds and estates detailed personal belongings better than any other source.[19] Because every artist and writer has a

14. Inventory of Alexander Telfair (1833). Chatham County Probate Court Records. (All wills and estate inventories cited hereafter are located in the Chatham County Probate Court Records unless otherwise noted.)

15. Richard Richardson sale (1822), Chatham County Court Records, *Deeds Book 2L, 1821–1823.*

16. *Columbian Museum and Savannah Daily Gazette* (August 9, 1817).

17. Richard Richardson sale (1822) and sale of furnishings by Archibald Bulloch, Chatham County Court Records, *Deeds Book 2L, 1821–1823.*

18. Gillow and Company Designs, Box W14B, Item E-48-1952 (Department of Prints and Drawings, Victoria and Albert Museum).

19. To dine—that is, to take dinner in an elegant, elaborate, or formal manner—is opportuned only to a select few. The dining elite possesses

point of view and a purpose, each reference holds the potential for special insights and misleading lapses. Only by consciously considering biases and reconfirming information in different sources does one approach an acceptable interpretation of dining in nineteenth-century Georgia.

Whenever possible, in both essay and catalog entries, the focus has been Georgia, Savannah, and the Telfair family. Sources from farther afield, such as books published in the North or England, came into play only when local or regional materials were not available. To complement the

---

wealth, the accoutrements of the table, and genteel bearing. Secreted away in the archives of the Chatham County Courthouse are estate records that give some of the best evidence about the stations and possessions of Savannahians long gone to dust.

A selection of forty-two inventories and thirteen related documents, including wills and records of sales, yielded twenty-six individuals who had met the prerequisites of occupation, wealth, and possessions deemed essential to membership in Savannah's upper class. These criteria were vocation as a professional, planter, factor, spinster, or widow; estate value exceeding $3,000; and possession of at least seven of the following ten items indicative of status and education: sideboard; teaware (ceramic, britannia ware, or silver); ceramic dinner set; silver (flatware and/or hollowware); forks; table linens; specialized glassware for entertaining; liquor, wines, or cordials; slaves; and books. Seven of the forty-two inventories boasted each of the ten status items: William Gibbons (1804), Edward Telfair (1808), Barack Gibbons (1814), George Haig (1816), Joseph Habersham (1832), John Williamson (1843), and Henry McAlpin (1851). Four inventories included nine of the ten items: Joseph Clay (1805), Joseph Bryan (1813), Isaiah Davenport (1828), and Priscilla Houstoun (1837). Ten listed eight items: John Gibbons (1816), John Courvoisie (1817), Francis Doyle (1817), Noble Wimberly Jones (1819), Charlotte Ann Palmer (1821), Benedict Bourquin (1822), Philip Brosch (1825), Sarah Blacksell (1825), Delia Bryan (1827), and John Screven (1831). Five included seven items: Thomas Telfair (1818), John Barnard (1827), Nicholas Bayard (1828), Alexander Telfair (1833), and Richard Wylly Habersham (1842). Sixteen inventories listed six or fewer items on the status list.

Crucial though they are to examinations of material culture, estate inventories are far from objective and often defy attempts to categorize decedents. Inherent biases toward the older, wealthier segment of society do not necessarily mar the study of an elite group, especially when life expectancy hovered around fifty years during the period in question. However, the inconsistencies in recording among the various scribes endlessly frustrates the researcher. Two factors peculiar to the South further diminish the value of estate inventories in categorizing its denizens. First, Southerners often owned town properties as well as numerous plantation properties, so that equally detailed inventories of all holdings are rarely found in the files of one probate court. Second, possession of slaves pushed up the net worth of some decedents with rather modest household belongings, so that wealth alone did not always correlate well with ownership of high status items. For instance, Thomas Potter, who was worth $191,534, mustered only six status items, while Edward Telfair and Joseph Habersham, worth slightly over $5,000 each, had all ten. From what we know of these individuals from other sources, it seems likely that not all of Potter's things or all of Telfair's assets appeared in the estate accounting of the Chatham County Probate Court.

Information from other sources and the multitude of variables that had an impact on the estate documents made rigid application of status criteria seem foolish. For example, some individuals, such as the baker Philip Brosch, who met neither the occupational nor estate value criteria, owned eight of the status objects, far more than some people with estates worth much more money. Sarah Telfair, the widow of Edward Telfair, who had owned all ten items, possessed only five status items. Did she distribute possessions to children before her death? Perplexing lapses in estate documents are explained occasionally by outside information. Alexander Telfair, the owner of a mansion and many luxurious objects, lacked a sideboard. Is it because Telfair shared his home with two maiden sisters and a widowed sister, Sarah Haig, who had inherited a fine sideboard from another brother?

The interpretation of inventories in this study makes no pretense to science. The criteria of status were far too broadly drawn and loosely applied to a small sampling of documents to make such a claim. It is left to someone with far greater resources to randomly select a statistical sample and devise

nineteenth-century ambience of the Telfair dining room, the text preserves in quotations the literary style and language of contemporaneous observers when it is feasible. Similarly, original spellings communicate the flavor of the era and have been kept with parenthetical clarification where necessary.

As recently as 1985 the dean of Georgia historians, Phinizy Spalding, asked: "Where, for example, is the permanent record of Georgia's cabinetmakers and ironworkers; its brick masons and architects; its painters and silversmiths? The answer, sadly, is nowhere. Their story has yet to be chronicled or their feats heralded."[20]

Through its holdings in architecture and decorative arts, the Telfair is beginning to explore and interpret life in nineteenth-century Savannah. By exhibiting and interpreting the objects in its care, the museum hopes to encourage inquiry into the field, so that Professor Spalding's question will find responses.

---

tighter categories. In the meantime this sampling of inventories enhances a beginning inquiry into the nature of elite dining in Savannah between 1800 and 1850.

20. Georgia Museum of Art, *Georgia's Legacy: History Charted Through the Arts* (1985), p. 23.

Part One

Nostrums for Fashionable Entertainments

DINING IN GEORGIA, 1800–1850

I. The Prospect

Hail! Sweet Savannah, Heav'n selected spot,
Whose taste combines the palace and the cot.[1]
Unknown, 1855

FROM THE SPIRE OF the Exchange Building, Firmin Cerveau looked south down Bull Street across Church Square and beyond, where the street became a road (fig. 7). The city spread before him, orderly as a chessboard; its white stucco and red brick buildings reflected the clear light of a May morning. Horses cantering along Bay Street kicked up only small puffs of dust, evidence that a recent rain had cleared the air.

Not far from the artist's perch, a black woman balancing a load on her head crosses Bull Street. Men carrying walking sticks and women in white bonnets stroll beneath Pride of India trees toward Washington Gardens at the head of Bay Street. There W. Cass sells ice cream, mead, cordials, and pastry.[2] At Bull Street and Bay Lane servants cluster, half hidden by the trees, around the door of Oyster Hall. Inside restaurateur William Luddington fills their masters' orders for oysters and oversees the kitchen.[3] Shrinking shadows tell the hour is 11 A.M. Turtle soup is simmering at the City Hotel, just west of Bull on Bay Street, and the day's pies—oyster, mincemeat, cranberry, and apple—are baking at Fechaux's American Restaurant, near the Exchange.[4]

Bed quilts stretched over hoops shade wagons filled with

1. Unattributed quote in Joseph Frederick Waring, *Cerveau's Savannah* (1973), p. 4.
2. *The Georgian and Evening Advertiser* (May 4, 1821), p. 3
3. *The Georgian* (October 13, 1832), p. 1.
4. *The Savannah Georgian* (November 15, 1830), p. 3; and *The Georgian* (November 14, 1821), p. 1.

Fig. 7. Firmin Cerveau, *View of Savannah* (1837). (Courtesy of the Georgia Historical Society.)

country produce.[5] Rolling toward the sheds of the city market, they creak past boys gamboling and cows lolling in the street. Convenient to the market is the new Gibbons Range. With a spirit that defied the devastation of the 1820 fire, young William Gibbons trimmed the brick building in elegant brown sandstone pilasters capped with Corinthian capitals carved from cypress. Browsers and buyers patronize Mr. Chamberlain at number five for crockery, china, and glassware, and the druggist, Mr. Parsons at number eight, to select newly imported teas.[6] Nearby on Broughton Street, "The Little Man's Garden" offers fresh seeds for sale.[7]

Bay Street bustles with people about their morning affairs. Flanking the intersection with Bull Street are the whitewashed facade of *The Savannah Georgian*, three doors to the left, and the bookstore-*cum*-private reading room of William T. Williams, three doors to the right. Together they account for the vitality of the printed word in the city. Men cluster in the doorway and on the brick sidewalk outside the newspaper office to learn the latest news or, more likely, to place announcements. Everyone—the grocer, the book-

5. Waring, p. 16.

6. *The Savannah Georgian* (May 21, 1825), p. 3; and *The Savannah Republican* (October 13, 1825), p. 1.

7. *The Daily Georgian* (February 14, 1821), p. 1.

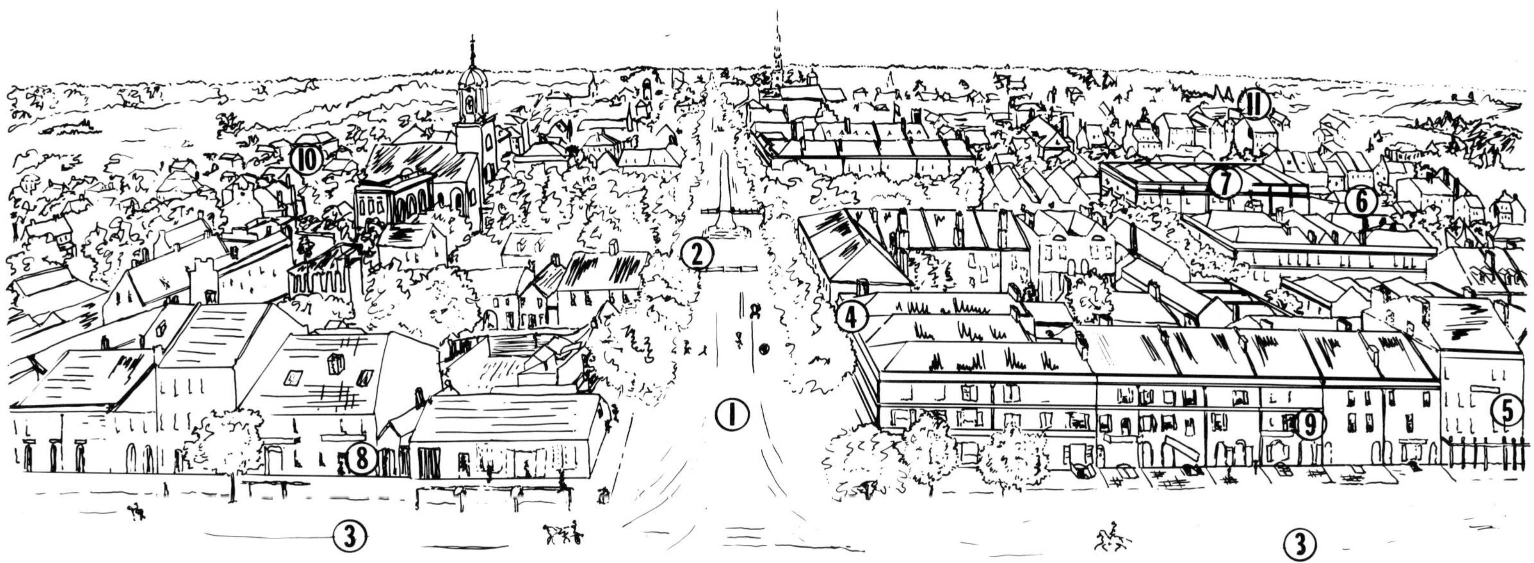

FIG. 7A. Schematic drawing of Firmin Cerveau's *View of Savannah* (*opposite page*). Cerveau placed the marble monument in Church Square (2) at the center of the painting, with Bull Street (1) bisecting the composition vertically. Bay Street (3) extends across the lower foreground. Oyster Hall (4) is at Bull Street and Bay Lane. On West Bay Street—that is, to the right of Bull Street—are William T. Williams's Bookstore and Reading Room (9), four buildings from the corner; and the white, four-storey City Hotel (5), three buildings farther west. The Gibbons Range (7) is the eight-bay, brick building west of Church Square. The city market (6) adjoins the western end of the Gibbons Range. The upper storey and roof of the Telfair house (11) are visible at the western edge of town. On East Bay Street—that is, to the left of Bull Street—is the office of the *Savannah Georgian* (8) in the two-storey building closest to the corner of Bull Street. The upper-storey and roof of the Richardson (now Richardson-Owens-Thomas) House (10) appear as the largest domestic building on the eastern edge of town. (Drawing by Stacey Swigert.)

seller, the innkeeper—publicizes goods and services in *The Savannah Georgian*. Mr. Williams carries a full range of literature and periodicals. Perhaps the slender figure entering his arched doorway is looking for a volume that he advertised, such as the second American edition of *Willich's Domestic Encyclopedia*.[8]

Shop signs show that businesses outnumber dwellings in the older section of town bordering the bay, but cottages with kitchen gardens still dot the area, while newer, richer dwellings wind around the squares in the south of town. Smoke rising from the chimney tops signals that preparations below are proceeding toward the 2 P.M. dinner hour, when families and friends gather for the day's main repast.

This was Savannah on a spring morning in 1837, just over one hundred years after Oglethorpe landed on the bluffs of the river to establish Georgia, the last of the original thirteen colonies. Now a little city of over ten thousand souls, Savannah remained unchallenged as Georgia's largest mu-

8. *The Georgian and Evening Advertiser* (April 10, 1821), p. 1.

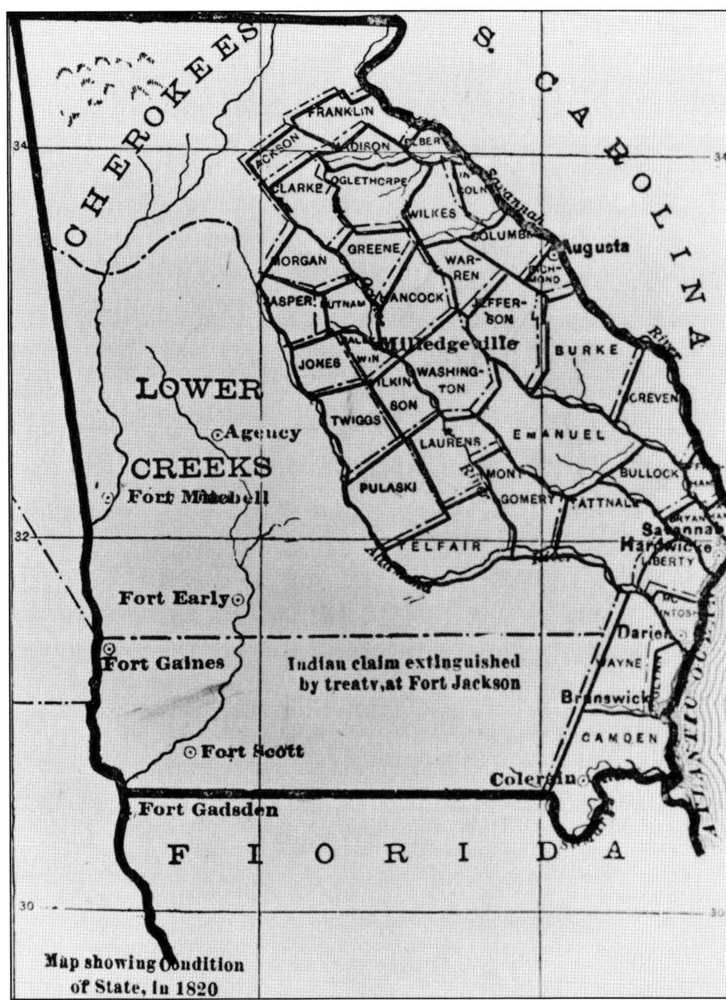

Fig. 8. "Map showing Condition of State, in 1820," from G. G. Smith, *Story of Georgia and the Georgia People, 1732–1860,* 2nd ed. (1901). (Courtesy of the Georgia Historical Society.)

nicipality, even though new settlers were entering the state and pushing the frontier westward. Although excluded from Cerveau's composition, the river, with its warehouses, wharves, and ships, had been and would remain the primary conduit of the city's prosperity and culture.

During the previous century Georgia floundered and the original colonists struggled to survive from 1733 until the Trustees surrendered their charter to the crown in 1752. The administration of the royal governors brought a modicum of prosperity to the young colony, but after twenty years the American Revolution disrupted the cadence of growth. When the nineteenth century opened, Georgia still lacked the accoutrements of civilization that older colonies had attained much earlier. In 1800 Indian Territory occupied more than half of the area now known as Georgia (fig. 8). White settlers sparsely populated the coastal region and a strip of land extending north and west between the Altamaha/Oconee and Savannah rivers. Villages—Augusta, Darien, Sunbury—grew up along the waterways as way stations for forest products and rice destined for export from Savannah.

Throughout the first half of the nineteenth century, the busy harbor continually enhanced Savannah's preeminent position as Georgia's largest commercial center. With the invention of the cotton gin in 1790, raising cotton had become profitable for Georgia planters. Increasing numbers of bales destined for distant mills passed through the port each year. The lively cotton trade linked Savannah factors both commercially and culturally to upcountry planters, on one hand, and to New York bankers and English manufacturers, on the other. English goods and customs continued to appeal to Savannah's white residents, most of whom were first generation emigrants from the British Isles or their descendants. At the same time, emerging American culture and native foods enriched long-standing English traditions.

While cotton generated wealth for Savannah and the hinterlands, it also held the seeds of decline. Growers tied up great sums in slaves and new land because the cultivation of cotton demanded intensive labor and quickly exhausted the soil. These capital requirements tended to keep Georgia sparsely populated and to retard the development of industry in the state. Equally portentous, the cotton grower's dependence on slavery helped to fuel the sectional divisions that finally erupted in the Civil War. Further, the middle decades of the century brought railroads to the fore in Georgia. The advent of reliable, overland transportation benefited landlocked urban developments that would rival and eventually surpass Savannah as Georgia's largest metropolis.

II. Provisions

Here almost every eatable thing can be found.
Emily Burke, 1850

FOREIGNERS VISITING the United States early in the nineteenth century unfailingly commented on the bounty of the American table. In a characteristic account, the Englishman Thomas Hamilton effused: "The table, instead of displaying, as with us, a mere beggarly account of fish and soup, exhibits an array of dishes closely wedged in triple column, which it would require at least an acre of mahogany to deploy into line."[9]

The image of abundance quickly became part of the American identity and began to appear in our national symbols. For example, depictions of Columbia often include a horn of plenty. Sheaves of wheat and fruit- and flower-filled baskets became popular motifs (see Part Two, catalog entries 14j, 14l, 14m). Consistent with these images, nineteenth-century Georgia offered a great variety of eatables. As Georgia's first city and only major port, Savannah stood at a crossroads linking the interior farmland and wilderness with the world beyond. Gathering in the harvest of the earth and the prizes of the hunt, as well as delicacies from abroad, Savannah overflowed like a cornucopia.

Many town households drew supplies of fruits, meats, seafood, and vegetables from nearby plantations. Production beyond the needs of home consumption was shared with neighbors or sold at the Savannah city market. Slaves allowed to raise animals and cultivate their own plots attained sales of about $100,000 annually in pigs, poultry,

9. Thomas Hamilton, *Men and Manners in America* (1833), 1:118.

fish, and vegetables.[10] Emily Burke was a New England schoolmarm who spent several years in Georgia. Recalling the Savannah city market (fig. 9), she observed:

> Here almost every eatable thing can be found. Vegetables fresh from the garden are sold the year round. All kinds of fish, both shell and finny, may be had there; birds of all kinds, both tame and wild, and the most delicious tropical fruits, as well as those which are brought from old countries. People travel a great distance for the purpose of buying and selling in the market.[11]

For poor country folk that meant as much as a three-day journey walking behind carts laden with truck to sell in Savannah.[12] Thanks to his scientific rather than epicurean interests, Charles Lyell commented on some meat for sale in the Savannah city market that was unfamiliar to him: "In the course of all my travels, I had never seen one opossum in the woods, nor a single raccoon, their habits being nocturnal, yet we saw an abundant supply of both of them for sale in the market here. The negroes relish them much."[13] In order to enhance the fresh food in the market,

FIG. 9. "The Public Market" [city market], from *The Industries of Savannah* (Savannah, 1886). (Courtesy of the Georgia Historical Society.)

urban merchants carried a full range of groceries imported from the West Indies, New England, and Europe, while specialty cooks readily supplied delicacies to those who could afford them.

The most basic source of food, Georgia's earth, yielded the fruit of many native shrubs and vines. General Horry of coastal South Carolina noted in his diary in June 1812 that the servants had gathered huckleberries, plums, blackberries, and mulberries for his dinner.[14] Wild fruit was eaten fresh, as well as canned for later use. Myrtie Candler

10. William A. Byrne, "The Burden and Heat of the Day: Slavery and Servitude in Savannah, 1733–1865" (Ph.D. diss. Florida State University, 1979), p. 124.

11. Emily P. Burke, *Reminiscences of Georgia* (1850), p. 21. The abundance of pineapples and bananas in the market was also a reminder of Savannah's proximity to the West Indies. See Sir Charles Lyell, *A Second Visit to the United States of North America* (1849), 2:7.

12. Frederick Law Olmsted, *The Cotton Kingdom: . . .* (1953), pp. 179–180.

13. Lyell, 2:7. Both slave narratives and archaeological evidence confirm the presence of opossums and raccoons in the Afro-American diet. Archaeological evidence further suggests that opossums and raccoons, albeit in lesser numbers, appeared on the tables of overseers and planters. See John S. Otto, *Cannon's Point Plantation, . . .* (1984), pp. 172–173; and George P. Rawick, ed., *The American Slave: . . .* (1972–1979), *passim*.

14. A. S. Salley, "Journal of General Peter Horry," in *South Carolina Historical and Genealogical Magazine, 38*, 3 (July 1937), p. 82.

remembered "the woods were full of blackberries, dewberries, and wild grapes and plums. Quantities would be picked and made into jam in the large copper kettle which was kept scoured to a brilliant glow with lye soap and wood ashes."[15]

From the time of the first colonists, American game was renowned as one of the staples of the table. As he journeyed through the South Carolina forests to take his post at a plantation near Savannah, the English tutor John Davis commented, "A dinner of venison, and a pint of Madeira, made me forget I had walked 30 miles."[16] Davis' description of life on the plantation is a hunter's idyll:

> The woods abound with deer, the hunting of which forms the chief diversion of the Planters. . . . William Henry [Davis' pupil] was an interesting lad of fourteen, ingenuous of disposition, and a stranger to fear. He was fond to excess of the chase. . . . I generally accompanied my pupil into the woods in his shooting excursions, determined both to make havoc among birds and beasts of every description. Sometimes we fired in volleys at the flocks of doves that frequent the corn fields; sometimes we discharged our pieces at the wild geese, whose empty cackling betrayed them; and once we brought down some paroquets that were directing their course over our heads to *Georgia*. Nor was it an undelightful task to fire at the squirrels on the tops of the highest trees, who, however artful, could seldom elude the shot of my eager companion.[17]

15. Myrtie Long Candler, "Reminiscences of Life in Georgia During the 1850s and 60s," in *Georgia Historical Quarterly*, *33*, 2 (June 1949), p. 118.

16. John Davis, *Travels of Four Years and a Half in The United States* . . . (1909), p. 65.

17. *Ibid.*, pp. 80–81, 85, and 90–91.

Charles Rinaldo Floyd, a Georgian who lived near St. Mary's, often mentioned hunting expeditions in the diary he kept between 1816 and 1845. Wild turkey, ducks, geese, larks, wild shoats, deer, rabbits, even jackdaws and bear cubs, fell before the guns of Floyd and his companions.[18] Recalling the abundance of Georgia's woods and waters and finding it conducive to cheerfulness and healthful life, Frederick Law Olmsted wrote about a dinner of game: "Two lads, the sons of my host, had returned the night before from a 'marooning party,' with a boat-load of venison, wildfowl, and fish; and at dinner this evening there were delicacies which are to be had in perfection, it is said, nowhere else than on this coast."[19]

Early Georgia settlers believed the land was most productive as range for cattle and hogs. In a tract written to encourage migration to Georgia, George Sibbald described the practice:

> The woods present a scene as new, as it is useful and delightful; an extensive forest, covered with high grass having all the appearance and reality of the advantage of a meadow, here the animals roam at large and are fit for the butcher, nine months of the year and remain in good order during the winter season, without any attention whatever.[20]

18. Charles Rinaldo Floyd, Diary, 1816–1845 (Manuscript Collection 257, Georgia Historical Society).

19. Olmsted, p. 178.

20. George Sibbald, *Notes and Observations, on the Pinelands of Georgia*, . . . (1801), p. 20. A contemporary view of cattle in the Old South tones down the rosy cast of Sibbald's promotional literature. Milk for human consumption was sometimes difficult to obtain from half-wild cows, and

Because cattle were allowed to range free, they were not always rounded up easily.[21] The 1814 estate inventory of Barack Gibbons made at Beech Forest Plantation, Chatham County, lists "46 Head of Cattle at $5—$230; 20 said to be in the woods $3—$60."[22] In order to provide beef for the table, cattle were at times hunted down by the hounds.[23] In his diary Charles R. Floyd recorded shooting a wild, large, black barrow; wild heifer; veal; steer; and other animals.[24] These entries in Floyd's diary refer to hunting feral animals, whose descendants still inhabit the islands of coastal Georgia.

In the low country the produce of the rivers and ocean came to the table regularly (fig. 10). Jeremiah Evarts recited the bill of fare on Daufuskie Island as being: "Beef steak broiled, an[d] others fried, three times a day; cold ham and sliced corn beef also at every meal. Often stewed and roasted oysters, boiled and fried fresh fish, crabs, shrimps."[25] Emily Burke also remarked on the abundance of fish in the low-country diet:

> The white fish, black fish, and even the catfish, came upon the table as frequently as any other; shellfish, such as crab, shrimp, and prawns, were more salable than those with fins. Oyster banks were very numerous; rising out of the rivers like a ledge of rocks, and where these banks occur near the plantations the slaves are able to add a very valuable article of diet to their otherwise coarse food.[26]

FIG. 10. "M. M. Sullivan, ". . . Shad, Fresh and Salt Water Fish, . . ." from *Haddock's Savannah Georgia Directory and General Advertiser 1870* (Savannah, 1871). (Courtesy of the American Antiquarian Society.)

General Horry of South Carolina sprinkled his diary, kept in the summer of 1812, with references to seafood destined for the table. One day Horry noted he had ordered his boat to be repaired so that he could have shrimp as well as local fish—croakers, mullet, whiting, catfish—for the table. Because it was difficult to preserve fresh foods, meals had to be carefully planned if the diners were not to be disappointed. General Horry's entry for July 24, 1812, records a regretful miscalculation: "Tide very low and no boat can come up the basin with fish time enough for dinner. I must arrange this

natural forage only produced fair livestock. See Sam Bowers Hilliard, *Hog Meat and Hoecake*, . . . (1972), pp. 112–140.

21. Olmsted, p. 179; and inventory of Priscilla Houstoun (1837).

22. Inventory of Barack Gibbons (1814).

23. Burke, p. 127.

24. Charles Rinaldo Floyd, Diary, 1816–1845.

25. Jeremiah Evarts, Diary, April 5, 1822 (Manuscript Collection 240, Georgia Historical Society).

26. Burke, pp. 139–140.

matter better—myself however eats little or no fish except oysters, clams and stone crabs and turpins [terrapins] which makes a good stew, or broth and their eaggs are mighty good eating."[27] From the tone of his diary, it seems that General Horry never turned down a turtle egg.

While wild plants and animals were important food sources for nineteenth-century Georgians, cultivated gardens and domesticated animals provided the core of the diet. A growing season extending from early March until late November gave Georgians an almost continuous yield of garden produce.[28] No doubt Daniel Mulford's sister in New Jersey was impressed when she read his letter written in Savannah on May 12, 1810: "Sallad and cabbage we have here all the year round. Green peas and green beans we have had for several weeks, as well as new irish potatoes:*This moment is the hight of the season for blackberries. Horse plumps begin to come and huckleberries and early peaches will be ripe next month."[29]

In addition to a major cash crop, such as rice, cotton, or corn, plantations produced a profusion of vegetables, herbs, and fruit for the table. According to advertisements placed in Savannah newspapers between 1810 and 1825, merchants offered a large selection of seeds to the gardener. Seed producers ranged from Messrs. John Fraser and Son, Botanist, of Chelsea, near London, to A. M'Mahon of Philadelphia, who advertised seeds "expressly for this market"[30] and presumably for the climate. Many items—including peas, turnips, cabbage, radishes, onions, lettuce, beans, celery, spinach, carrots, cauliflower, and sorrel—came in two or more varieties. Seed for leeks, beets, asparagus, artichokes, nasturtium, marjoram, garlic, horseradish, mustard, sage, basil, and savory were also sold. By the 1830's books such as H. L. Barnum's *Family Receipts or the Practical Guide for the Husbandman and Housewife* (1831) gave instructions for cultivating most of these and other plants. However, for skeptics who suspect that seeds are not necessarily the harbingers of harvest, Myrtie Candler's description of a Middle-Georgia plantation garden should suffice:

> Through the garden ran a long walk with a grape arbor over it bearing scuppernongs and grapes. In this garden were beds of vegetables with walks between. . . . There was a permanent asparagus bed that produced mightily, and a strawberry bed, and there were raspberries and artichokes in addition to beans, peas, okra, tomatoes, cucumbers, lettuce and other vegetables that grow so well in Georgia. . . . Some distance away and out of sight, were the various "patches." The roasting ear patch, the potato patch, the turnip patch, the watermelon and muskmelon patches. . . . In the vegetable garden were bushes of all kinds of seasoning herbs,—sage, sweet basil, thyme, sweet marjoram, coriander, calamus, horseradish, leeks, onions, garlic—that I remember.[31]

Because homegrown foodstuffs sustained a large work force on many plantations, some garden vegetables were grown as field crops. The "potato patch" was, no doubt, a field for growing sweet potatoes, which, along with corn,

27. Salley, *39*, 1 (January 1938), p. 47.

28. Hilliard, p. 173.

29. Daniel Mulford letter to Betsey Crane, May 12, 1810 (Manuscript Collection 579, Georgia Historical Society).

30. *The Republican and Savannah News Ledger* (February 3, 1810), p. 3; and *The Savannah Georgian* (March 26, 1825), p. 1.

31. Candler, *33*, 2 (June 1949), p. 116.

turnips, peas, and melons, were a primary staple of the slave diet.

Mrs. Candler alluded to several kinds of fruit trees cultivated in Georgia, saying:

> In the summer quantities of fruit was dried; for in the winter ahead there would be pies, turnovers and tarts to make, and stewed fruit every day. Sheets of white cloth would be stretched in the sun. Peaches, apples, pears, and figs would be prepared and carefully laid on these sheets. When they were well dried they were put away in stone jars and sealed.[32]

The diversity of garden produce matched the variety of livestock raised on the plantation. "The poultry yards were full to overflowing, and the woods teemed with numerous herds of cattle, horses, mules, and goats, while scores of red and yellow swine literally turned up the meadows in search of worms."[33] Only a few Chatham County estate inventories listed flocks of poultry.[34] Where they did appear, however, the ubiquitous chicken or fowl was almost equalled in numbers by turkeys, geese, and ducks. Noted in eighty percent of the Chatham County inventories containing livestock, sheep were far more common than poultry in the estate documents examined for this study. While sheep were raised for fleece, mutton and lamb were not rarities on Georgia tables.[35] For example, Aaron Burr listed mutton among the plentiful foodstuffs on one Georgia plantation, and even so punctilious a critic as Fanny Kemble found the mutton flavorful.[36] Herds of cattle furnished milk and beef for the table; however, meat was preserved by less than perfect methods in Emily Burke's judgment:

> Meat is not salted or barrelled as here, but smoked and dried, and generally tainted during the process. I never saw any meat preserved in this way that I could eat; and it was more than I wished to do, to sit at the table where it was. I was once passing a corn-house on a plantation with a servant woman where I observed the smell of putrid flesh; on making inquiry what it was, the woman informed me that it was beef drying upon the top of the house; for they dry all their meat in the summer, when they can have the benefit of a good hot July or August sun.[37]

Myrtie Candler recalled that "outside in the yard over the barbecue pit, the shoats and kids were cooked by two men, one basting while the other turned the spit."[38] According to Emily Burke, Georgians raised goats solely for the flesh of kids that was considered preferable to lamb. The perceived superiority of kid may have rested on its scarcity relative to lamb, for only fifteen percent of the sample inventories containing livestock documented goats.[39] Regard-

32. *Ibid.*, p. 118.

33. Burke, p. 119.

34. Inventories of Barack Gibbons (1814) and Noble W. Jones (1819). While our sample of inventories records far less poultry than livestock, travelers' accounts confirm that poultry came frequently to the table. See Hilliard, pp. 46–47.

35. The inventories of Barack Gibbons (1814) and his heir, Noble W. Jones (1819), differentiate between common and merino sheep. At $30 a head, Barack Gibbons' merinos were considerably more valuable than his common sheep enumerated at $3 each.

36. Matthew L. Davis, *Memoirs of Aaron Burr* (1837), 2:333; Hilliard, pp. 45–46.

37. Burke, pp. 26–27.

38. Candler, *33*, 3 (September 1949), p. 224.

39. Inventories of William Gibbons (1804), Joseph Clay (1805), and Noble W. Jones (1819).

less of the comparative popularity of all other meats, pork stood unchallenged in its prominence on the Georgia table. Burke explained:

> As it respects the swine, I believe the people of the south would not think they could subsist without their flesh; bacon, instead of bread, seems to be their staff of life. Consequently, you see bacon upon a southern table, three times a day, either boiled or fried. This custom of course demands the slaughter of a great number of these animals on every plantation during the year. On the one of which I am speaking in this communication, during the fall I was there, one hundred passed under the butcher's knife at one time, and all for home consumption. I will leave my New England friends, who know well what a disturbance the butchering of one of those noisy creatures creates with us, to judge what a scene would be occasioned by the collecting together and massacre of one hundred at a time.[40]

A center of trade, Savannah welcomed ships from many ports. Packets from Charleston, New York, Philadelphia, Boston, and other American cities called only a little more regularly than ships from the West Indies, Liverpool, Hamburg, and other European ports. Savannah newspapers advertised cargoes of eatables that rivaled the diversity of locally produced foods. The firm of Wilson & Knox placed this typical advertisement for a basic staple: "from Charleston and will be sold cheap if applied for soon. Two thousand five hundred lb. Green Coffee in bags."[41] Chests of fresh Hyson and Imperial tea entered the port (fig. 11). Sugar of various types, such as muscavado and Havana, came in dif-

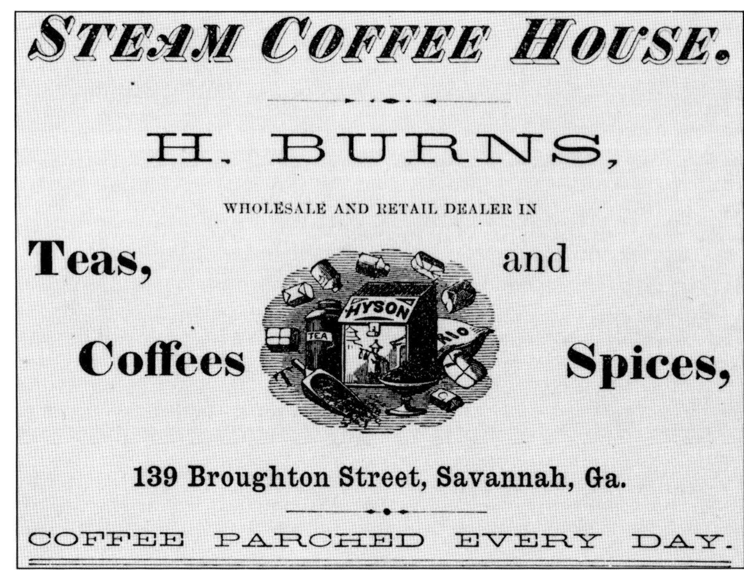

Fig. 11. "Steam Coffee House. H. Burns, . . . Teas, Coffees and Spices," from *Estill's Savannah Directory for 1874–1875* (Savannah, 1875). (Courtesy of the American Antiquarian Society.)

ferent forms—for example, loaf, lump—and quantities—for example, hogsheads and barrels. Not all sugar was imported. In 1815 John McNish advertised: "Georgia Sugars. The subscriber has just received and offered for sale ninety-five hogsheads SUGAR, made by Thomas Spalding, esq. of Sapelo Island, equal if not superior in quality to any imported from the West Indies."[42] Merchants also sold Spalding's molasses by the hogshead. One could purchase fresh, superfine flour by the whole and half barrels as well as buckwheat meal and ready-made baked goods, such as Bremen rolls, Hyslop's crackers, butter biscuits, pilot and midding

40. Burke, pp. 222–223.

41. *The Georgia Republican and State Intelligencer* (May 12, 1803), p. 1.

42. *The Savannah Republican and State Intelligencer* (April 18, 1815), p. 4.

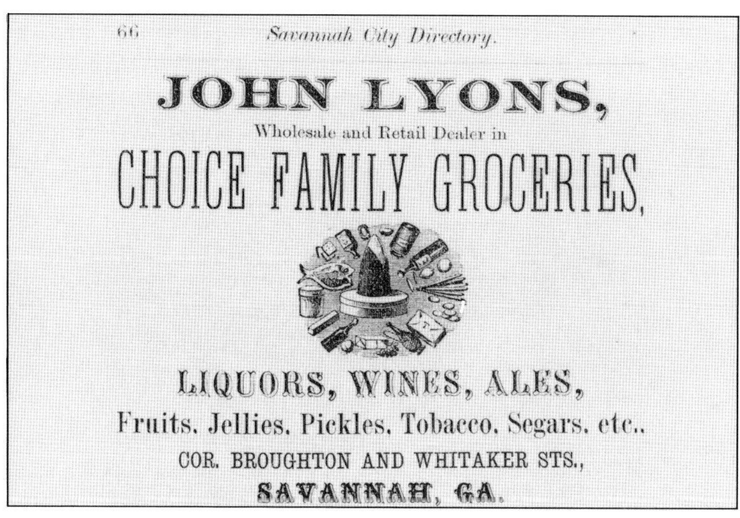

FIG. 12. "John Lyons, . . . Choice Family Groceries, Liquors, Wines, Ales, . . ." from *Directory of the City of Savannah for 1870* (Savannah, 1870). (Courtesy of the Yale University Library.)

bread. Other starchy staples included new white beans, green peas, split peas, pearl barley, and vermicelli.

Savannahians could provision their larders with imported meats, such as bologna sausages, pickled tongues, corned beef, and smoked beef from New York. In 1810 merchants advertised barrels of New York mess and prime beef; but by 1825 it was known as Fulton Market beef, named after the main meat exchange in New York City. In spite of the local supply, Savannah retailers imported bacon, Baltimore hams, and other pork products. Kegs, barrels, boxes, and quintals of smoked and pickled salmon, smoked and pickled herring, plain and corned codfish, Northern shad, and mackerel augmented local seafood.

Except for onions and Irish potatoes, which travel well, vegetables were rarely shipped to Savannah from afar. Some fresh fruit arrived from the North, including pears, cranberries, and apples. "Pippin" was such a well-known term that advertisers announced the arrival of fall pippins rather than apples. Sweet oranges came from the West Indies. Bunches of raisins (muscatels and blooms); barrels of soft-shelled almonds; kegs of currants; best turkey figs; and fresh prunes might round out a stock of fruit (fig. 12).

Relatively few dairy products could be shipped successfully during the first quarter of the nineteenth century. Dutch producers, however, sent Edam and Gouda cheeses to Savannah. Philadelphia and Goshen butter as well as Goshen cheese were commonly available.

The selection of imported sweetmeats and condiments sounds particularly exotic and luxurious to the modern reader. In 1810 Peter Morin announced:

> The Subscriber Has just received a complete assortment of the best SWEETMEATS ever imported here, some of which are entirely new, and of the most exquisite taste, such as Guava Jelly, Ditto Paste, Do. Mamlet, Micada in boxes of one pound each. PRESERVES Pine Apples, Limes, Lemons, Zoronga, Sidra, Ycacoa, Tamatidos in pots. Tamarinds and sweetmeats. ON HAND Currant, Quince, Apple and Strawberry Jellies, and all kinds of Brandy Fruits. In order to accommodate his customers, he will sell his Sweetmeats either by the jar or by a single pound, on moderate terms.[43]

43. *The Republican and Savannah News Ledger* (March 15, 1810), p. 3. Given the tropical origin of most of the fruits and the use of Spanish words, the shipment announced here probably came from a Hispanic port in the Caribbean. Mamlet is probably marmalade; Micada is a paste made with sweetened coconut meat; zoronga and sidra are misspellings of the Spanish words for grapefruit and citrus. Likewise, Ycacoa and Tamatidos (probably Tomatillos) are tropical fruits.

FIG. 13. "J. N. Muller, Importer of and Wholesale Dealer in German and French Wines, . . ." from *Directory of the City of Savannah for 1870* (Savannah, 1870). (Courtesy of the Yale University Library.)

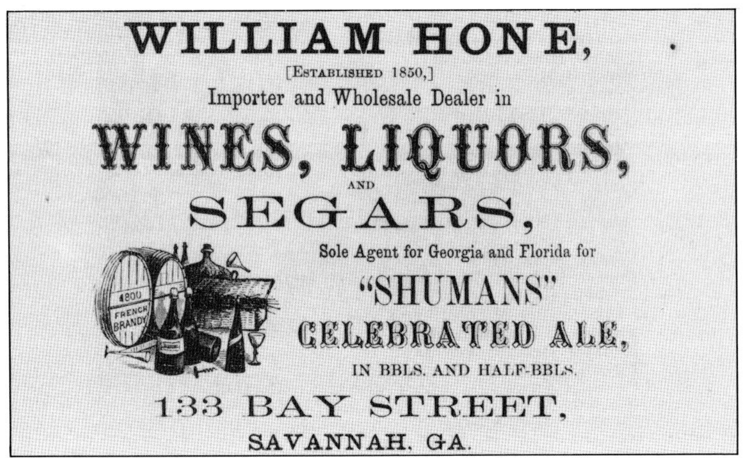

FIG. 14. "William Hone, . . . Wines, Liquors, and Segars, . . ." from *Directory of the City of Savannah for 1870* (Savannah, 1870). (Courtesy of the Yale University Library.)

Walter Roe's notice of groceries and liquors just received from Charleston and New York included "Green Guages, Cherries, Pears, Apricots, Peaches etc., in brandy and in syrup. A very handsome Assortment of Confectionary. Preserved Citrons, in six pound boxes."[44] Vendors also publicized double-refined liquorice and best New York chocolate.

The thirty-four nutmegs entered in William Gibbons' estate inventory are emblematic of the importance of spices in nineteenth-century life.[45] Savannah purveyors distributed a full range of spices—from cloves, nutmeg, ginger, mace, cinnamon, and aniseeds, to black pepper, cayenne pepper, curry, arrowroot, pimento, ginger, basket and Liverpool salt. Since condiments provided obligatory accompaniments to most meals, merchants stocked ready-made London pickles and mustards, mushroom and walnut ketchups, and fish sauces as well as raw materials such as anchovies; capers; olives; sweet oil; wine vinegar; wine bitter; orange flower water and rosewater, double distilled.

No meal was complete without proper beverages, so Savannah grocers sold liquors in addition to foodstuffs (fig. 13). George Lewis' advertisement names products that would accommodate a typical range of tastes:

> Bay Lane, nearly opposite the exchange, offers for sale low for cash only, The Following Good Things: Jamaica shrub, warranted by the gallon or bottle; real Holland gin; real Northern gin; old cognac brandy; real wine vinegar; Port, Claret and Cattaloquia wines, on draught or bottled; London Porter and excellent Newark Cider, on draught; . . . N. B. families can be supplied with ex-

44. *The Republican and Savannah Evening Ledger* (January 16, 1810), p. 4.

45. Inventory of William Gibbons (1804).

cellent spruce beer as above, by sending 6 1/4 cents and an empty bottle.[46]

Lewis and other merchants advertised ciders—London, Philadelphia, Crab, and others—but according to Daniel Mulford's observations, it was not a tremendously popular item. In a letter dated October 16, 1810, he wrote to his sister in New Jersey:

> We have fine, large, fall pippins, excellent for eating, plenty in market. Cider also begins to come and will soon be very low. As for cider spirits, very little of it is ever brot here. The people are fonder of their own corn whiskey. But should spirits be sent, as I think some will, the first that arrives could not bring more than 4/ or 5/ per gallon, and should much arrive it would not bring half a dollar. The people of this country are astonishingly prejudiced against it. They even prefer Yankee rum.[47]

Savannahians who preferred whiskey could augment their domestic brew with everything from Jamaican, West Indian, and New England rum to Georgia fourth proof rum and North Carolina corn whiskey. By 1825 Old Kentucky Whiskey was sold in Savannah as well. In addition to London and Philadelphia porter, Savannah merchants carried Albany beer, English ale, and American brown stout (fig. 14). Since liquids were often retailed by the pipe (125 gallons), it is not surprising to find sixty gallons of rum in the estate inventory of Edward Telfair and five dozen jugs of porter in the inventory of William Gibbons.[48]

At his death in 1832 Alexander Telfair's wine cellar contained 714 bottles and eighteen gallons of wine, in addition to 152 empty bottles.[49] Most of Alexander Telfair's wines were Madeiras, but there was also sherry, port, and scuppernong wine. Claret and rhenish—that is, French and German—wine as well as very old cognac and peach brandy appeared in Savannah shops. Essential to elegant dinners, many cordials were produced at home, but some such as peppermint cordial and cherry and raspberry ratafia were sold by grocers.

In 1805 Frederic Tudor established an enterprise to export New England ice to Southern climes. Perhaps it is only a coincidence that on April 23, 1806, the following announcement appeared in *The Columbian Museum and Savannah Advertiser*:

> The *Ice House Committee* will, on Monday next, deliver the rated proportion of Ice to such of the subscribers ONLY as have paid the first amount demanded of them, together with the additional requisition. The time of delivery will be from half past six to seven o'clock a.m. The house will not be opened at any other hours.[50]

Although Tudor is reputed to have created the demand for ice in the United States, in 1823 refrigeration was still not foremost in the minds of those Savannahians who did not escape to the North for the summer.[51] Their disinterest spurred the notice that follows:

46. *The Republican and Savannah Evening Ledger* (May 25, 1815), p. 1.
47. Daniel Mulford letter to Betsey Crane, October 16, 1810 (Manuscript Collection 579, Georgia Historical Society).
48. Inventories of Edward Telfair (1808) and William Gibbons (1804).
49. Inventory of Alexander Telfair (1833).
50. *The Columbian Museum and Savannah Advertiser* (April 23, 1806), p. 3.
51. Daniel J. Boorstin, *The Americans: The National Experience* (1965), p. 12.

> Savannah Ice House. The owners of this establishment having met with so little encouragement the last summer, will be compelled to close it the ensuing season, unless a sufficient number of subscribers can be obtained to meet the expenses, etc., of the establishment. A subscription paper will be opened in a few days, to ascertain whether the owners can be warranted in supplying the house with ice the present winter.[52]

Orders increased, so the proprietors replenished the icehouse for the summer of 1824. Other evidence confirms that ice was becoming a necessity. The 1824 estate inventory of Gardner Tufts registered a ten-dollar icehouse.[53] Further, fromages, which had to be chilled with ice, were prominent desserts in a handwritten, Telfair family recipe book dating from around 1825. The anonymous author penned in this comment: "Fromages require they must be very delicate, but above all very cold."[54]

Although most dishes were prepared at home, professional cooks found a market for specialty foods. One advertisement announced: "Mock Turtle Soup will be dressed on Saturday next, at LEAH SIMPSON'S, in the white house, in Fahm Street, opposite Mr. Newell's mills. Families can be supplied by sending between 11 and 12 o'clock. Decent accommodations for gentlemen disposed to call."[55] For those more inclined toward the real thing, "a fine, fat, Bahama green Turtle will be dressed on Tuesday next, at 11 o'clock by SYLVIA WAITFIELD on the bay. Families supplied by sending."[56]

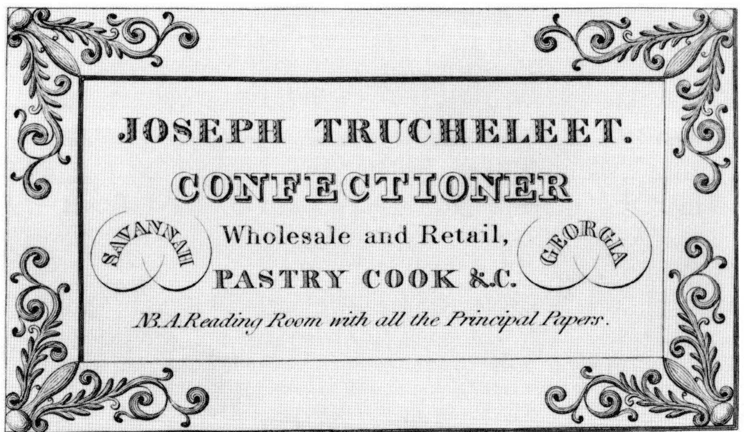

Fig. 15. Trade card of Joseph Trucheleet *[sic]*, from Joshua Shaw, *United States Directory for the Use of Travellers and Merchants* [1822]. (Courtesy of the Henry Francis du Pont Winterthur Museum Library: Collection of Printed Books and Periodicals.)

Between 1815 and 1825 the professional cooks of Savannah counted a number of Frenchmen in their ranks. One was a confectioner whose trade card appeared in Shaw's *United States Directory*: "Joseph Trucheleet [*sic*], confectioner, wholesale and retail, pastry cook, etc. . . ." (fig. 15). With his slaves, Guilliaume the cook and James the baker, manning the kitchen, Truchelut turned his hand to promoting and expanding the confectionary enterprise. Astutely anticipating a profit from the patriotic and Francophile sentiments generated by Lafayette's visit, Truchelut illuminated his shop on the night Savannah honored the revolu-

52. *The Daily Georgian* (December 19, 1823), p. 3.

53. Inventory of Gardner Tufts (1824). Icehouses valued at $17 and $3 were entered in the inventories of William Gaston (1837) and John Williamson (1843), respectively. A considerably more expensive ice machine ($200) appeared in the inventory of Joseph Stiles (1839).

54. Paperbound recipe book (Manuscript Collection 793, Georgia Historical Society).

55. *The Republican and Savannah News Ledger* (March 15, 1810), p. 3. Mock turtle soup is made with beef rather than turtle.

56. *The Republican and Savannah Evening Ledger* (May 20, 1815), p. 4.

tionary hero with a reception. In addition he filled his show glasses with imports from France—china tea sets, colognes, pickles, preserved fruits, cordials, and clarets.

Other enterprising Frenchmen were the owner and chef, Messrs. Fechaux and Daregne, of the "American Restaurant." Fechaux advertised that his chef was "well known in the first Hotels in New York, Augusta, and at Saratoga Springs as a first rate cook and excellent pastry maker."[57] Hopefully Fechaux did not purvey the chicken pie that Mrs. David Hillhouse disdained in her account of a Savannah dinner party: "At the head of the table was a large, flat, chicken pie with one fowl only, which the lady of the house informed us was made by one of the best French cooks in America and that it cost four dollars."[58]

In the first half of the nineteenth century, Savannah reigned as a commercial center and enjoyed the best of local produce and imported foodstuffs. On the other hand, the small towns of middle Georgia existed in isolation. Poor transportation restricted the range of groceries available in towns like Sparta. Daniel Mulford lamented in a letter written to his brother in New Jersey: "Sparta afforded nothing suitable or at all effectual in raising me to health. Hog, hominy and collards are the substantials of diet and very little but substantials could be found. Not a woman in the village knew how to make me a piece of cake."[59]

In a letter to his sister Betsey Crane, Mulford elaborated on the women of Sparta:

> They live in a part of the country where pear leash is seldom sold and they know very little of any other means of raising bread, their choicest articles for tea etc. are little biscuits baked in a pye pan. Ovens are seldom used, and of course they have no baked bread but what is baked in a pye pan and is miserable stuff. Collards which you inquire about, is a coarse kind of cabbage, which never heads.[60]

Town dwellers and small landholders in the backcountry lacked luxuries that self-sufficiency and access to markets brought to wealthy planters. While planters dined, the common farmer and his slaves returned from the fields to the house where they sat on the floor together and shared a meal of hominy from one dish.[61]

57. *The Georgian* (November 14, 1821), p. 1.

58. Marion Alexander Boggs, *The Alexander Letters, 1787–1900* (1980), p. 50.

59. Daniel Mulford letter to Levi Mulford, Savannah, January 10, 1810 (Manuscript Collection 597, Georgia Historical Society).

60. Daniel Mulford letter to Betsey Crane, Savannah, May 12, 1810 (Manuscript Collection 597, Georgia Historical Society).

61. Burke, pp. 21–22. For a well-documented overview of provisions with an emphasis on agriculture, see Hilliard, *Hog Meat and Hoecake*.

III. Food Preparation

How all these things could be cooked would puzzle a Northern man to tell.
Jeremiah Evarts, 1822

IN WELL-TO-DO households such as the Telfairs', slaves labored to turn the bounty of the land into feasts for the table. During a visit to Daufuskie Island, near Savannah, Jeremiah Evarts wrote this commentary on his host's table:

> There are always a number of visitors and generally some retainers. Food is provided in most abundant of quantities and in great variety. I observed not fewer than ten or twelve hot dishes for breakfast and supper, besides many cold ones. These dishes were generally excellent in their kinds. . . . How all these things could be cooked would puzzle a Northern man to tell. I was once in the kitchen, and could not see half utensils enough to cook a common article with ease. Yet the cooking was always well done, and with great regularity as to time. Slaves have few conveniences for any kind of labor. They are obliged to do everything by the hardest.[62]

Around 1810 cookstoves began to supplant open-hearth cooking in the Northeast.[63] However, open-hearth and brick-oven cooking methods remained dominant in the kitchens of Georgia slave-owners at least until the end of the Civil War.[64] Consequently Evarts was not alone in his

62. Jeremiah Evarts, Diary, April 5, 1822 (Manuscript Collection 240, Georgia Historical Society).

63. Priscilla J. Brewer, "'We Have Got a Very Good Cooking Stove,'—Advertising, Design, and Consumer Response to the Cookstove, 1815–1880," in *Winterthur Portfolio* (Fall 1990), p. 35.

64. In interviews recorded during the 1930's, Afro-Americans raised on Georgia plantations often recollected hearth cooking and the absence of cookstoves in plantation kitchens. His 1851 inventory marked Henry McAlpin as the only Savannahian in our study who owned a cooking stove, and he possessed two. The one at his town house was valued at $4.50 while

view that no modern conveniences alleviated the slave cook's daily toil. Almost thirty years later Emily Burke wrote in a similar vein about cooks in Southern kitchens:

> Of all the house-servants, I thought the task of a cook was the most laborious. Though she did no other housework she was obliged to do everything belonging to the kitchen department, and that, too, with none of those conveniences without which a northern woman would think it impossible for her to prepare a meal of victuals. After having cooked the supper and washed the dishes she goes about making preparations for the next morning's meal. . . . In the morning she is obliged to rise very early, for she has every article of food that comes onto the table to cook, nothing ever being prepared till the hour it is needed. When she has gone through with all the duties connected with the morning's repast, then she goes about the dinner. . . . In this manner the cook spends her days, for in whatever department the slaves are educated, they are generally obliged to wear out their lives.[65]

Miss Burke concluded, however, that she often thought the mistress of the house was the greater slave, for she was obliged to weigh and measure every commodity that passed into the hands of the cook as slaves were not considered trustworthy.[66] Many slaveholders kept everything under lock and key.[67]

Preconceptions about service, slavery, race, and human nature colored writers' interpretations of the competence and working conditions of domestic slaves. Where some saw nothing but degradation, others found inspiration in extraordinary individuals who rose above adversity. Thomas Hamilton, an English visitor to New York, took a dim view of all American servants, both hirelings and slaves. He lamented that an American matron was her own housekeeper and attended to petty details. In the same vein Hamilton bluntly stated that a butler was out of the question in an American household. The master would rather have had his wine cellar keys at the bottom of the Hudson River than in the hands of "black Caesar."[68] Cruel gibes made at the expense of slaves who tried so hard to please her diminish Fanny Kemble's stature in spite of the moral high ground she took in opposing slavery.[69] Conflicting feelings about servitude and race also crop up in the contradictory observations of the English author, Mrs. Basil Hall: "The nasty, black creatures whom they have for servants" deprive Southerners' parties of style, she asserted.[70] Four pages later she admired a dinner where "the whole establishment

the one at the Hermitage Plantation was worth twice as much, $9. See Ronald G. Killion and Charles Waller, *Slavery Time When I Was Chillun Down on Marster's Plantation* (1973), pp. 8, 15, 32, 105; and George P. Rawick, *The American Slave . . .*, vol. 12, pt. 1 (1976), p. 217; and vol. 13, pt. 1, p. 3.

65. Burke, pp. 123–124. Born a slave in Georgia in 1855, Jennie Kendricks corroborated Burke's views when she recalled: "As [my] Grandmother did all of the cooking, none of the other servants ever had to cook, not even on Sundays or other holidays such as the Fourth of July. There was no stove in this plantation kitchen, all the cooking was done at the large fireplace where there were a number of hooks called potracks" (Rawick, vol. 13, pt. 1, p. 3).

66. For a contemporary interpretation of the mistress as "the slave of slaves" that emphasizes a link between sexual and racial oppression, see Catherine Clinton, *The Plantation Mistress, . . .* (1982).

67. Burke, pp. 153–154.

68. Hamilton, 1:116.

69. Frances Anne Kemble, *Journal of a Residence on a Georgian Plantation in 1838–1839* (1961), pp. 60–61, 253.

70. Mrs. Basil Hall, *The Aristocratic Journey, . . .* (1931), p. 217.

is apparently under the most excellent management; all the servants, although slaves, born and bred, a race whom we have generally found so stupid, understand their business perfectly."[71] Even Mrs. Hall might have acknowledged that Frederick Law Olmsted's assessment reasonably accounts for some discrepancies among observations: "Really well-trained, accomplished, and docile house-servants are seldom to be purchased or hired at the South, though they are found in old wealthy families rather oftener than first-rate English or French servants are in the North."[72]

While it is indisputable that all American servants did not measure up to the highest English standard, numerous observers contradict negative assessments with accounts of well-schooled and thoroughly competent slaves who served as waiters, butlers, and cooks in Southern households. Tyrone Power expressed a positive view shared by many Northern and foreign visitors to Savannah.[73] He recalled: "My days were passed at the hospitable home of Mr. G——n, where I encountered many pleasant people; and was attended by the sleekest, merriest set of negroes imaginable, most of whom had grown old or were born in their master's house: his own good-humoured, active benevolence of spirit was reflected in the faces of his servants."[74]

71. *Ibid.*, p. 221.

72. Olmsted, p. 98.

73. William A. Byrne, "The Burden and the Heat of the Day: . . ." (1979), p. 107.

74. Mills B. Lane, ed., *The Rambler in Georgia* (1973), pp. 69–70. Fredrika Bremer also saw the good temper and kindness of her Savannah host mirrored in his slaves; see Fredrika Bremer, *The Homes of the New World: . . .* (1853), 1:363.

Those destined to become domestic slaves were often the offspring of house servants, so learning how to perform household duties began early as the child followed its mother or mistress around the master's home. Because skills were acquired in the time-honored ways children have always learned to "help" their elders, specific methods of training domestic slaves receive little notice in literature. Therefore, former slaves asked in the 1930's to look back seventy years give some of the best accounts of childhood tutelage. Since a clever adult can almost always make a chore into a game, the former slave Anna Parkes recalled that "All chilluns done wuz to frolic and play. I was jes' 'lowed ter tote de key basket. . . ."[75] More common tasks for children included carrying wood, sweeping, watching younger children, arising with their mothers at 4 A.M. to help in the kitchen, fanning flies, and waiting on the table.[76] Nellie Smith is representative of most of the former slaves living in the 1930's. She recollected: "I was jus' gittin' big enough to handle that old peafowl-tail fly brush they used to keep the flies off the table when we were set free."[77] Slavery ended before her generation experienced what might have been a more rigorous apprenticeship of a young adult.

Most domestic slaves undoubtedly received all of their training in their masters' households; some slave-owners, however, did seek the polish of specialized schooling for

75. Rawick, vol. 13, pt. 3, p. 157.

76. Rawick, vol. 12, pt. 1, pp. 80, 316, 319; pt. 2, pp. 195–196; and vol. 13, pt. 3, pp. 88, 309; pt. 4, p. 179. See also Killion and Waller, pp. 32, 104, 118.

77. Rawick, vol. 13, pt. 3, p. 309.

their servants. For children of slave-owners experienced in instructing servants, the matter was no more complicated than sending the servant home to mother and father. Wanting his slave George to retain his training and acquire a "house look," the Savannahian Charles C. Jones, Jr., asked his father if it would be convenient to take George into his household.[78] Others who could afford it sent their servants farther afield. The widow Favors paid the owner of a hotel four hundred dollars to have the hotel chef teach her slave cook how "to prepare all kinds of fancy dishes."[79] Likewise owners committed fledging waiters, valets, and butlers to an apprenticeship of several years with Lee at the clubhouse in Charleston and were well pleased by the results.[80] Regrettably details of the training and feats of these highly skilled waiters, butlers, and cooks are lost in their virtual anonymity, save a snippet here and there.

First and foremost, slave cooks prepared meals by European techniques to please European palettes, but foods and practices drawn from African tradition also entered into their repertoires. African slaves usually arrived in the New World with some knowledge of native crops because Europeans had introduced American plants—maize, yuca, sweet potatoes, peanuts, red peppers, and sugar cane—to Africa beginning in the sixteenth century.[81] Likewise Afro-Asian cultigens—rice, yams, okra, cowpeas, sesame, sorghams, and millets—and domestic animals—cattle, sheep, goats, swine, and fowl—were also familiar commodities in Southern kitchens.[82] Through the intermingling of African, American, and European elements, slave cooks prepared their feasts for the table.

Southerners boasted about the excellence of their cooks; moreover, at least two compared well to European counterparts. Born in Savannah, but best known as an arbiter of New York society, Ward McAllister devised an entertainment to prove that New Yorkers who ordered dinners from a caterer could fare as well as Savannahians who had a family cook in the kitchen. His sixty guests gathered at a dinner in Newport to rank the capacities of a Southern cook and a French chef. Given the premise of the competition, it's not surprising that McAllister believed the French chef came off the victor, but he had to concede that "both were great artists in their way"—the black cook, with his wonderful natural taste, excelling at making things savory.[83]

Before Willy and Daisy Low moved to England, they were well known in Savannah for the excellent dinners prepared by their cook, Mosianna Milledge. After experiencing difficulties with English servants, the Lows persuaded her to come to England. In time the Lows added a journeyman English cook to the household staff. There Mosianna Milledge taught the now legendary Rosa Lewis to prepare many of the delicacies that won her favor with the Prince of Wales and his circle—rice, sweet potatoes, waffles, Virginia hams,

78. Robert M. Myers, ed., *The Children of Pride: . . .* (1972), p. 427.

79. Rawick, vol. 12, pt. 1, p. 320.

80. J. H. Easterby, ed., *The South Carolina Rice Plantation as Revealed in the Papers of Robert F. W. Allston* (1945), pp. 33, 123. Although mentioned twice in the Allston letters, Lee is not identified by surname or details other than those given.

81. Otto, p. 85.

82. *Ibid.*

83. Ward McAllister, *Society as I Have Found It* (1975), pp. 99–101.

canvas-back ducks, turkey, terrapin soup, brandied peaches, and sweet corn.[84]

Even among the first-rate servants of Savannah, the Telfair slaves stood out. In each generation family members wrote wills manumitting slaves who had served them well.[85] Of the thirty-five slaves entered in the 1833 inventory of Alexander Telfair, the most highly valued was Friday.[86] One of seven house servants, Friday undoubtedly acted as the Telfair's butler.[87] In a letter to Margaret Telfair Hodgson, Louisa McAllister recalled a domestic scene in the Telfair household. She mused: "I think of you and dear Mary and would gladly find myself sitting by the fire in the dear Oak Room where even now I can see you all with Friday bringing in the tea tray and your little Page in devoted attendance."[88] Mary Telfair provided another glimpse of her house servants on the eve of one of her tours of Europe (*ca.* 1842–1855), when she wrote a friend to arrange for their employment during her absence. She recommended Juddy as a cook:

> She has been ours for some years past, and is an excellent tempered woman, and strictly honest, one who can be trusted with your keys. . . . Her daughter Coomba is a chamber Maid, and an elegant clear starcher. She is delicate in constitution, and very neat in her habits, the wife of George. . . . George, who though inferior to Friday in smartness, you would find very honest, steady and faithful. . . . He can make Mrs. Habersham's Cake, Charlotte Russe, but not puff paste. We shall be very glad as they are an affectionate trio to have them domesticated with you.[89]

Friday accompanied the Telfairs to Europe.

If the facts of slavery in Georgia and Southern mythology ever converged, it was in the homes shared by a few aristocrats like the Telfairs and their personal servants.[90] The obituary of William Brown Hodgson, which appeared in the *New York Home Journal*, noted that he had "married into the wealthy and honored family of the Telfairs, of Savannah, whose well known consideration for their inherited

84. Martha Giddens Nesbit, "English Taste Buds Influenced by Savannah?," in *Savannah Morning News* (December 6, 1978).

85. Names of family members, year of death, and number of slaves freed are as follows: Sarah Gibbons Telfair, 1827, 5; her brother, William Gibbons, 1804, 3 (also left property to previously freed slaves); her first cousin, John Gibbons, 1816, 53 (left property to some slaves); her son-in-law, George Haig, 1816, 1 ("for his faithful services to me").

86. Friday was Alexander Telfair's most valuable slave, but as a general rule slaves with technical skills—drivers, coopers, blacksmiths, carpenters, engineers, and so forth—received the higher appraisals than house servants.

87. Inventory of Alexander Telfair (1833). Telfair's inventory does not list occupational titles. In inventories and documents where they do appear, typical titles for domestics include butler, valet, cook, waiter or footman, chambermaid, seamstress, nurse, laundress, gardener, and coachman. In the majority of households most servants did more than one job.

88. Louisa McAllister letter to Margaret Telfair Hodgson, December 5, [no year] (Manuscript Collection 793, Georgia Historical Society). The writer was Ward McAllister's mother. Recalling her visit to Savannah, Amelia Murray described a similar scene: "A lady here has taken great pains with a negro boy born in her family. I was amused to see him standing behind her chair, with a tray under his arm, like a little black statue" (quoted in Byrne, p. 173).

89. Mary Telfair letter to William [no surname], [n.d.] (Manuscript Collection 793, Georgia Historical Society).

90. Byrne, p. 166.

Africans has associated their names with humanity."[91] A few vignettes recorded in the letters of Mary Telfair illustrate that humanity was the key; by acknowledging the humanity of their slaves, the Telfairs demonstrated their own.

Whether the service she desired involved traveling one thousand miles to summer in the North or simply stepping across the room to snuff a candle, Mary Telfair remembered to consider the feelings of her servants. She mentioned to a friend that she was relieved to hear Juddy tell "her comrades here [in Savannah] that she was very much pleased with her northern summer—everybody was kind to her. I hope that it will be an inducement to her to repeat it—we never compel any of them to do what will make them unhappy."[92] On another occasion she wanted to write more, but Mary Telfair closed her letter abruptly because her valet was waiting to put out the candles.[93] Although accounts of Christmas celebrations turn up repeatedly in slave narratives, it seems the practice of the Telfair household was not repeated elsewhere. In most households all slaves had the day off, except the cook and waiters who prepared and served the master's feast for family and friends. The Telfairs always declined invitations to Christmas dinner because, as Mary Telfair noted: "It is the custom with us to cook a large dinner for our servants[;] each has the privilege of inviting their friends—so they keep the festival and are made happy by it."[94] Haunted by the loss of close relatives, Mary Telfair described returning home after a long absence: "No cheerful voice to welcome us, but our Servants, who seemed quite overcome by the sight of us. . . . I never knew before how much they valued us."[95] While Mary was surprised, it was probably not a shock to anyone else that the Telfair servants appreciated their masters for the decent treatment they received and returned it in kind.

Although slaves carried out the kitchen labors, the mistress of the household, who bore responsibility for the table, closely supervised them. One English author lamented, "Gentlemen of moderate fortunes . . . , who marry women uninstructed in cooking and the management of a family, are objects of singular compassion."[96]

Luckily for their benighted husbands, ladies who had entered into marriage ill equipped for domestic endeavors could consult a number of sources for guidance in cooking and housekeeping. By the early nineteenth century English publishers exported quantities of books on cookery, conduct, and domestic management to the United States. Amelia Simmons, who billed herself as an American orphan, wrote the first American cookbook in 1796. It and other early American cookbooks were essentially recapitulations of English sources. The more comprehensive volumes instructed on everything from marketing, menus, recipes, and the

91. *New York Home Journal* (July 31, 1871).

92. Mary Telfair letter to Mary Few, November 16, [no year] (William Few Papers, Georgia Department of Archives and History).

93. Mary Telfair letter to Mary Few, March 29, [no year] (William Few Papers, Georgia Department of Archives and History).

94. Mary Telfair letter to Mary Few postmarked January 15, [no year] (William Few Papers, Georgia Department of Archives and History).

95. Mary Telfair letter to Mary Few postmarked December 12, [no year] (William Few Papers, Georgia Department of Archives and History).

96. John Armstrong, *The Young Woman's Guide to Virtue, Economy, and Happiness* [1817], p. vi.

rules of boiling and roasting to etiquette, carving, and home remedies. Regional cookbooks, such as *The Virginia Housewife* (1824) and *The Carolina House wife* (1847), which addressed issues of local cuisine, soon followed the encyclopedic directories into print. Certainly the most treasured resources were handwritten recipe books that were passed down in families from generation to generation.

Many reference books took a more theoretical than practical approach to cookery and dining. A typical volume, *Lectures on Diet and Regimen* (1800), by Anthony F. M. Willich, was in the Telfair family library.[97] Consistent with the early nineteenth-century vogue for everything classical, Willich proposed the regimen of the ancient Greeks as the most healthy way of life. He went on to hypothesize that yellow fever must stem from the "*vicious diet* and *incautious regimen* peculiar to Americans."[98] He supported his theory by arguing:

> Nor is the conclusion rash, when we find all foreigners, who visit this country, Frenchmen, Germans, and even Englishmen, exclaiming against *our copious* and *everlasting* dinners. Not that feasts and sumptuous entertainments are unknown in Europe, at which the rules of sobriety are trampled upon, but they are given on particular occasions only, where as the ordinary of an American is an everyday feast. Americans who have traveled abroad, know the truth of this observation. To indulge in a party, where excess must follow, once or twice a month, may hurt us; but to overload the stomach every day, must kill us in a short time.[99]

Willich sheds a good deal of light on foods of the period. For instance he suggests: "The most suitable ingredients of salads, besides lettuce, are the various cresses, chervil, (Chaerophyllum bulbosum, Cinn.) and the scurvey grass, which together with the other cooling herbs, produce the effect of cleansing the humours, or, as some say, of purifying the blood, and are at the same time diuretic; especially if eaten in Spring, and upon an empty stomach."[100]

Common sense underpins much of Willich's advice. He recommended taking exercise, brushing teeth, keeping clean, and avoiding patent medicines. Just when *Diet and Regimen* seems very up-to-date, a paragraph like the one on sugar crops up:

> It has been frequently asserted, that sugar injures the teeth: this, however, is not strictly true; for it is only by its vitiating the stomach, and generating impure blood, that the teeth become sympathetically affected. Hence persons of weak digestion, those with dibilitated nerves, the hypochondriac, hysteric women, and especially children subject to complaints arising from worms, ought to use this luxurious substance sparingly, and only occasionally.[101]

Another book from the Telfair family library is *Practical Hints to Young Females* (1816) by Mrs. Taylor. Again, the

97. The Boston edition of A. F. M. Willich's *Lectures on Diet and Regimen* found in the Telfair library was published in 1800. Perhaps an indicator that Willich found other readers in the South, Thomas Cooper, president of the South Carolina College, contributed additions to the 1821 Philadelphia edition of Willich's *Domestic Encyclopedia*. Consequently Anna Wells Rutledge includes it in "A Preliminary Checklist of South Carolina Cookbooks Published Before 1935, " in [Sarah Rutledge], *The Carolina Housewife* (1979), p. 224. Further, the Cooper edition of *The Domestic Encyclopedia* was advertised for sale by the Savannah bookseller W. T. Williams in *The Georgian and Evening Advertiser* (April 10, 1821), p. 1, col. 3.

98. A. F. M. Willich, *Lectures on Diet and Regimen* (1800), p. vii.

99. *Ibid.*

100. *Ibid.*, p. 81.

101. *Ibid.*, pp. 136–138.

focus of the book is more philosophical than practical. Chapter titles give insight into the daily concerns of the nineteenth-century lady—conduct to husband, domestic economy, servants, education, sickness, visitors, keeping at home, recreation, the stepmother. Mrs. Taylor observed:

> That house is well conducted, where there is a strict attention paid to order and regularity. To do everything in its proper time, to keep everything in its right place, and to use everything for its proper use, is the very essence of good management. . . . Meals should always be ready at the stated time; and servants if possible obligated to be punctual: but to effect this, and prevent confusion, they must receive clear and early orders.[102]

In concluding, Mrs. Taylor pronounced:

> There is certainly no part of domestic management which requires more skill and address, in order to unite gentility with economy, than the conduct of the table. . . . Those who are in the habit of frequenting genteel tables will learn, by proper observation, how to conduct their own, as to appearance and arrangement; and the culinary detail may be learned, as far as instruction can ever teach without practice, from a book, entitled *'A New System of Domestick Cookery; Founded on Principals of Economy, and Adapted to the Use of Private Families.* By a Lady.'[103]

First published in Boston in 1807, this book "by a Lady" (Mrs. Maria E. Rundell) enjoyed a wide distribution throughout the United States.[104] Like most of the Anglo-American books, it combined household tips and recipes. The title of *The Young Woman's Guide to Virtue, Economy, and Happiness* (1817) by John Armstrong implies a panacea for womankind lies within its pages. In fact, it contains over six hundred recipes, in addition to rules for reading with propriety and for conducting epistolary correspondences; sketches of history, geography, and astronomy; memoirs of illustrious females; the history of women; directions for domestic bookkeeping; cookery for the poor; the mode of covering the table; the art of carving; methods of potting, pickling, preserving, and so forth; bills of fare; instructions for the brewing of malt liquor and the making of choice British wines; advice to female servants; the choice of a husband; articles relating to family medicine; and last but not least, the mode of preserving and improving the beauty both of the shape and countenance.[105] Mrs. Farrar's *The Young Lady's Friend by a Lady* (1837) summarized the popularity of etiquette books in America: "[In a] society like ours, where the sudden acquisition of wealth brings families into new positions, and surrounds them with new associates; where talents and education carry people into the most refined circles, without any previous training in manners, it is very necessary to have some means of finding out what belongs to polished life."[106]

In her introduction to *The Carolina Housewife* Sarah Rutledge referred the reader to one of the exhaustive cookbooks as a source of general methodology. Then she presented the *raison d'être* of regional cookbooks, noting that:

> French and English Cookery Books are to be found in every book-store; but these are for French or English servants, and almost always require an apparatus either

102. Mrs. Taylor, *Practical Hints to Young Females* (1816), pp. 30–31.
103. *Ibid.*, pp. 106–107.
104. Mary Randolph, *The Virginia House-wife* (1984), p. 316.
105. Armstrong, pp. vii-xi.
106. [Eliza Ware (Rotch) Farrar], *The Young Lady's Friend by a Lady* (1837), pp. 346–347.

> beyond our reach or too complicated for our native cooks. The "Carolina Housewife" will contain principally receipts for dishes that have been made in our own homes, with no more elaborate *abattrie de cuisine* than that belonging to families of moderate income; even those dishes lately introduced among us have been successfully made by our own cooks.[107]

Further, Rutledge's book contained over one hundred recipes for dishes composed of rice, corn, okra, sweet potatoes, fresh seafood, and other local ingredients. Mary Randolph's *The Virginia House-wife* was a bellwether among regional cookbooks. She adapted traditional English cookery to the Virginia environment and to American customs. For example, Mrs. Randolph calculated her methods of butchering and preserving meat in order to achieve a maximum period of freshness in the hot, Virginia climate. The 1825 edition of *The Virginia House-wife* even included simple plans for a home refrigerator. Most of Mrs. Randolph's recipes, such as "Chicken Pudding, a favorite Virginia dish," were grounded in English practice, while others, such as "To Barbecue Shote," were purely Southern.[108]

Writing about Georgia for a Northern audience, Emily Burke explained that on special occasions large gatherings were "treated to a 'barbecue,' a term that means at the South, one or more swine roasted whole. These feasts are prepared and given in the woods in a most rural manner."[109] John Duncan, an Englishman, received an invitation to a barbecue in Virginia. He recalled:

> The spot selected for this rural festivity was a very suitable one. In a fine wood of oaks by the roadside we found a whole colony of black servants . . . busied with various processes of sylvan cookery. One was preparing a foul for the spit, another feeding a crackling fire which curled up round a large pot, others were broiling pigs, lamb, and venison over little square pits filled with red embers of hickory wood. From this last process the entertainment takes it name[110] (fig. 16).

The idea of roasting oysters, which originated with the Indians, so appealed to the white population of the low country that the oyster roast became an eagerly anticipated winter observance.[111] Writing about his youth, I. Jenkins Mikell recalled a Christmastide festivity one never declined—the annual oyster roast at Bleak Hall on Edisto Island, South Carolina. He began by describing the preparations of the woodland setting carried out the day preceding the party:

> Rustic tables and seats . . . were put in place. Cords of oak, hickory, and cedar—for the aroma—. . . were . . . placed ready for the torch. The "white foot" oysters were obtained a few yards from the "Camp" and left in salt water until the last minute so as to preserve their peculiar flavor and tang of the sea. . . . By sunrise [on the day of the party], wagons were moving, containing everything pertaining to an elaborate feast . . . accompanied by a host of household and kitchen servants. . . . At noon, the fire for the roast was started. At one o'clock when the guests arrived, the oysters were poured on the live coals . . . and were soon ready. The host arose. . . . Then

107. Sarah Rutledge, *The Carolina Housewife, . . .* (1979), p. iv.
108. Randolph, pp. 63, 99.
109. Burke, p. 199.
110. John M. Duncan, *Travels Through Part of the United States and Canada in 1818 and 1819* (1823), 1:296–297.
111. Sarah Rutledge, *The Carolina Housewife: . . .* (1979), p. xvii.

FIG. 16. William E. Wilson, *Barbecue, near Savannah* (*ca.* 1883–1889). (Courtesy of the Georgia Historical Society.)

> lifting his glass he simply said: "To our kinsfolk, our guests—welcome!" Immediately a dozen little picanninnies rushed from the fire with platters filled with hot, sputtering oysters and placed one before each person, and for a time nothing was heard save the knife struggling with an obdurate oyster. . . . Recess, and a stroll or ride along the beach was now in order [for dinner was only an hour away].[112]

In her introduction Sarah Rutledge implied that there would be no need for *The Carolina Housewife* if every young housekeeper inherited a handwritten recipe book from her grandmother. Aided by such a manuscript, any young lady could easily teach the cook to send up proper meals.[113] Judging from handwritten recipe books in the Telfair family papers, Mrs. Rutledge was correct in drawing a parallel between the *The Carolina Housewife* and collections of family recipes. Both eschew general methodology, stem from English tradition, and feature foods and techniques generated from the American experience.

112. Katherine M. Jones, *The Plantation South* (1957), pp. 228–229.
113. Rutledge, p. iv.

Numbering just over one hundred entries, the most extensive Telfair family recipe book dates between 1825 and 1830.[114] Titles—Ann W.'s Plumb Cake; Blackberry Jelly, Mrs. Haig's; Mrs. William Hunter's Mincemeat; Italian Cream, E. Clay's recipe; Angels Food, Mrs. George Jones; French cake furnished by Virginia Hunter—show that friends and relations shared their favorites. The instructions run the gamut from dressing salsify and pickling shad to instantaneous ginger beer and "stomacick tincture." A majority of the recipes, however, are for cakes, puddings, and other sweets. Most reflect a firmly English palate: English plum pudding, jumbles, queen cakes, gingerbread, bath buns, Tunbridge cakes, and so forth; but others embody an American outlook. There is ample use of cornmeal in Indian bread, griddle cakes, rye rolls, pancakes, and Indian pudding. Directions for watermelon rind pickles, blackberry jelly, stuffing turkey, pickling shad, pickling ham with red peppers, and smoking ham with hickory wood or corn cobs echo a distinctly American tone.

114. Paperbound recipe book (Manuscript Collection 793, Georgia Historical Society).

IV. American Manners

If you would be refined, you must avoid blowing your nose at the table.
Eliza Farrar, 1837

CLEARLY, ENGLISH PRECEDENT governed American dining. English travelers in the United States, however, considered Americans and their customs a great curiosity. Like most foreign writers, Thomas Hamilton admired the abundance of food in America. Then he continued:

> To be sure, if the devil sends cooks to any part of the world, it is to the United States, for in that country it is a rare thing to meet any dish dressed just as it ought [to] be. . . . The national propensity for grease is inordinate. It enters largely into the composition of every dish, and constitutes the sole ingredient of many. The very bread is, generally, not only impregnated with some unctuous substance, but when sent up to the breakfast table, is seen to float in a menstruum of oleaginous matter.[115]

Hamilton found the preparation of food no less obnoxious than the manners of his companions at a New York hotel:

> Around, I beheld [a] scene of gulping and swallowing, as if for a wager. . . . .In my own neighborhood there was no conversation. Each individual seemed to *pitchfork* his food down his gullet, without the smallest attention to

115. Hamilton, 2:6. Travelers, both foreign and American, lamented the greasy, monotonous fare served in hotels and inns, particularly those in remote places. Young W. R. Waring wrote his aunt this facetious account of the supper at a rural inn where he stopped enroute to college in Athens, Georgia: "I forgot to tell you what a fine supper Mr. Simmons gave us; it was a chicken fried, served up in a bowl half filled with melted lard which made a body think he was taking medicine, Delicious fried pan-cakes thin as a wafer cooked white instead of brown and with plenty of grease" (W. R. Waring letter to Mrs. G. J. Kollock, August 20, 1847 [Manuscript Collection 1275, Georgia Historical Society]).

> the wants of his neighbor. If you asked a gentleman to help you from any dish before him, he certainly complied, but in a manner that showed you had imposed on him a disagreeable office; and instead of a *slice*, your plate was generally returned loaded with a massive wedge of animal matter.[116]

Any man who did not carve skillfully without rising from his chair was exhibiting extremely poor form. Even ladies were expected to be able to carve. In *The Cook and Housekeeper's Complete and Universal Dictionary* (1822) Mary Eaton observed: "Some people haggle meat so much, as not to be able to help half dozen persons decently from a large tongue, or a sirloin of beef; and the dish goes away with the appearance of having been gnawed by dogs."[117] Like most cookbook authors, Mrs. Eaton offered a chapter of thorough instructions on carving and an admonition to practice (fig. 17).

Some American habits frowned on by the English received approbation from American arbiters of etiquette.[118] For instance, Mrs. Basil Hall commented unfavorably when

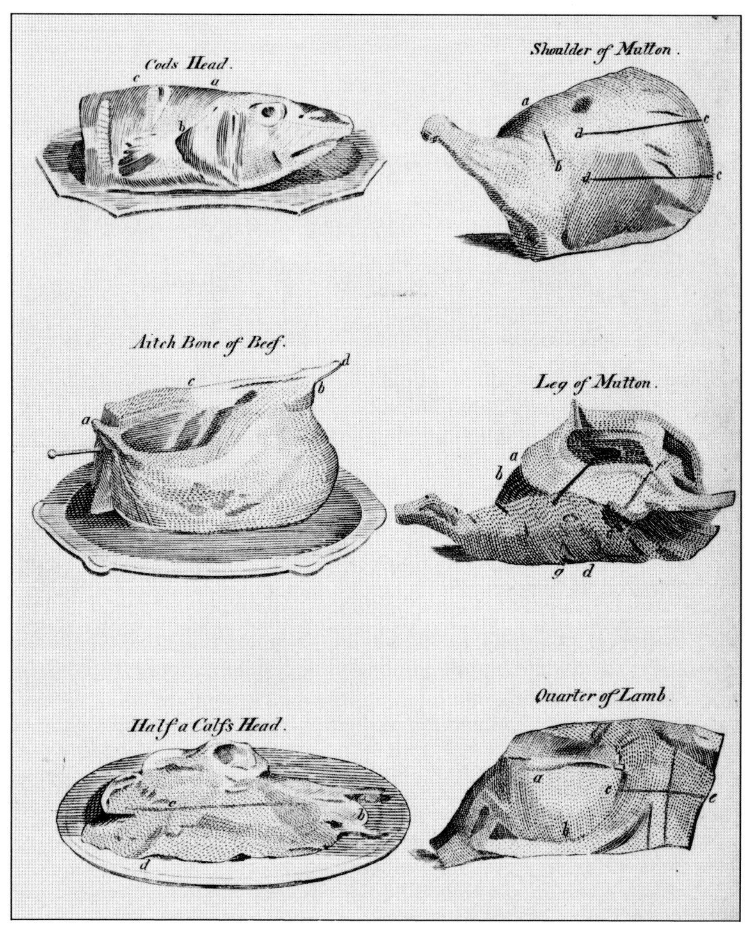

FIG. 17. Carving diagram showing cod's head, etc., from John Armstrong, *The Young Woman's Guide to Virtue, Economy, and Happiness* (Newcastle upon Tyne, [1817?]). (Courtesy of the Research Libraries, the New York Public Library.)

116. *Ibid.*, 2:43. Another Englishman, John Duncan, had passed some time in the United States before he was able to equal the velocity of his neighbors in dispatching their meals; and a third, James Stuart, commented that "the business of repletion went forward with a rapidity altogether unexampled" (Duncan, 1:319; and James Stuart, *Three Years in North America* [1833], 1:24).

117. Mary Eaton, *The Cook and Housekeeper's Complete and Universal Dictionary* (1822), p. xxix.

118. The nineteenth century brought prosperity and bourgeois aspirations to many Americans, creating an audience for manuals of genteel behavior. For a discussion of standards for all types of behavior including dining, see John F. Kasson, *Rudeness and Civility: Manners in Nineteenth-Century Urban America* (1990).

she saw Americans eating with their knives.[119] Yet, *The Young Ladies' Friend* advised:

> If you wish to imitate the French or English, you will put every mouthful into your mouth with your fork; but if you think, as I do, that Americans have as good a right to their own fashions as the inhabitants of any other country, you may choose the convenience of feeding yourself with your right hand, armed with a steel blade; and provided you do it neatly, and do not put in large mouthfuls, or close your lips tight over the blade, you ought not to be considered as eating ungenteelly.[120]

Even this author had to draw the line somewhere, so she cautioned: "If you would be very refined, you must avoid blowing your nose at the table."[121]

To describe the American manner of eating soft boiled eggs as lacking refinement would be too kind. Scarcely a single English visitor let it pass without comment, and Thomas Hamilton recorded the custom most graphically:

> Eggs, instead of being eat from the shell are poured into a wine glass, and after being duly and disgustingly churned up with butter and condiment, the mixture, according to its degree of fluidity, is forthwith either spooned into the mouth, or drunk off like a liquid. The advantage gained by this unpleasant process, I do not profess to be qualified to appreciate, but I can speak from experience to its sedative effect on the appetite of an unpracticed beholder.[122]

When English correspondents visited the South, they found kindred spirits. Even Thomas Hamilton was not offended by the conduct of the table at Jones's Hotel in Charleston.[123] There was no bolting or scrambling at dinner.[124] Hamilton rhapsodized: "The pleasure of getting into such a house,—of revisiting the glimpses of clean tablecloths and silver forks,—of exchanging salt pork and greasy corncakes, for a table furnished with luxuries of all sorts,—was very great."[125] The English tutor, John Davis, also found life very congenial in the deep woods of South Carolina. The table of his employer, Mr. Drayton, "was sumptuous, and an elegance of manners presided at it that might have vied with the high circles of polished Europe. I make the eulogium, or rather exhibit the character of Mr. Drayton, in one word, by saying he was a gentleman; for under that portraiture I comprehend whatever there is of honor."[126] Although Mrs. Basil Hall could not resist making some acerbic comments about the entertainments at Charleston, she had to admit that she was sorry she could not linger in Savannah.[127] Even this compliment was a bit backhanded because she rejoined it with "the greater number of our associates here [in Savannah] are English or

119. Helen Sprackling, *Customs of the Table Top: . . .* (1958), p. 15.

120. Farrar, pp. 346–347.

121. *Ibid.*, p. 347.

122. Hamilton, 2:25. Likewise, Duncan warned the reader that Americans "empty two half boiled eggs into a wine glass, and drink rather than eat them." Stuart also noted the custom. See Duncan, 1:319; and Stuart, 1:29.

123. Kept by a black family, the Jones's Hotel was also noted in Tyrone Power, *Impressions of America; During the Years 1833, 1834, and 1835* (1836), 2:56.

124. *Ibid.*, 1:278.

125. *Ibid.*

126. Davis, p. 82.

127. Mrs. Basil Hall, p. 227.

Scotch or connected with them, and this has made the society particularly pleasing to us." [128] On the other hand, William Makepeace Thackeray made no disclaimers. In a letter posted from Savannah he decreed:

> I write from the most comfortable quarters I have ever had in the United States. In a tranquil old city, wide-streeted, tree-planted, with a few cows and carriages toiling through the sandy road, a few happy negroes sauntering here and there, a red river with a tranquil little fleet of merchant-men taking in cargo, and tranquil ware-houses barricaded with packs of cotton,—no row, no tearing northern bustle, no ceaseless hotel racket, no crowds drinking at the bar,—. . . a famous good dinner, breakfast, etc., leisure all the morning to think and do and sleep and read as I like. The only place I s[t]ay in the States where I can get these comforts—all free gratis—is in the house of my friend Andrew Low. [129]

Both foreign visitors and Americans acknowledged that the manners of affluent Southerners were above average for the United States. In his *United States Directory for the Use of Travellers and Merchants* (1822), Joshua Shaw affirmed Charleston's claim to "the first rank in the Union for hospitality, generosity and urbanity." [130] He continued: "Savannah resembles Charleston in the manners of its inhabitants, the same attention to strangers, affability, hospitality and encouragement of literature alike distinguishing both cities." [131]

Born in nearby Beaufort, South Carolina, Bishop Stephen Elliott of the Diocese of Georgia spoke from a more intimate and longer standing acquaintance with Savannah than did the foreigner Shaw. Nevertheless, he drew similar conclusions. Looking back in 1866, Bishop Elliott confessed he had lived in Savannah only twenty-five years, but remembered "its society for full forty years, having visited it frequently during my boyhood and early manhood. Upon those visits, I was brought into contact with its cleverest men and I found among them a very high standard of literary excellence and of classical attainment." [132] Contending that cultivated society arose from a salubrious mix of intellectuals and those "who gathered around their hospitable boards all that was clever and refined," Elliott avowed that Savannah met the criteria. [133]

Thomas Hamilton found Northerners and Southerners diametrically opposed in disposition. Perhaps his comparison is a little overdrawn, but it aptly delineates differences in temperament that affected dining customs. Hamilton regarded the New Englander as:

> A man of regular and decorous habits, shrewd, intelligent, and persevering; phlegmatic in temperament, de-

128. *Ibid.*

129. William Makepeace Thackeray, *A Collection of Letters of Thackeray, 1847–1855* (1887).

130. Joshua Shaw, *United States Directory for the Use of Travellers and Merchants* [1822], p. 115. For an assessment of hospitality in Southern life, see Bertram Wyatt-Brown, *Southern Honor: Ethics and Behavior in the Old South* (1982), pp. 331–339.

131. *Ibid.* For a comparable view of the similarities between Charlestonians and Savannahians, see James Silk Buckingham, quoted in Mills B. Lane, ed., *The Rambler in Georgia* (1973), p. 139.

132. Waring, pp. 70–71.

133. *Ibid.*

> voted to the pursuits of gain, and envious of those who are more successful than himself. The [Southerner]—I speak of the opulent and educated—is distinguished by a high-mindedness, generosity, and hospitality. . . . He values money only for the enjoyments it can procure, is fond of gaiety, given to social pleasures, somewhat touchy and choleric, and as eager to avenge an insult as to show a kindness. In point of manner, the Southern gentlemen are decidedly superior to all others of the Union. Being more dependent on social intercourse, they are at greater pains perhaps to render it agreeable. There is more spirit and vivacity about them, and far less of that prudent caution, which, however advantageous on the exchange, is by no means prepossessing at the dinner-table, or in the drawing room.[134]

Two works of art depicting dining scenes illustrate beautifully Hamilton's point of view. *The Dinner Party* (fig. 18) by the Bostonian, Henry Sargent, and *Friends and Amateurs in Musick* (fig. 19) by the Charlestonian, Thomas Middleton, embody the attitudes of the painters, as well as reinforce Hamilton's description of regional temperaments.

Both painters chose to depict intimate scenes from their personal lives. *The Dinner Party* is a view of Sargent's own home at 10 Franklin Place.[135] Likewise, the scene in *Friends and Amateurs in Musick* can be presumed to be Middleton's home because one of the paintings in the drawing has been identified as the *Portrait of Thomas Middleton* by Benjamin West.[136] The painters' aims, however, were entirely different. True to Hamilton's assessment of the New Englander as shrewd and devoted to the pursuits of gain, Sargent painted his large canvas as an exhibition piece. He sold it to an entrepreneur who charged admission for a glimpse of upper-class life that might appeal to curious audiences aspiring to greater wealth. Middleton conceived his drawing as a private memento of a habitual gathering of friends.

Each artist elected to show a moment near the end of a dinner after a servant had removed the tablecloth. While Sargent has portrayed a convivial scene, it still reflects the decorum expected of a Bostonian. All is orderly, from the table top to the seating of the company. Even Sargent's symmetrical frame of the composition and neatly placed, fashionable furnishings reveal a penchant for propriety. On the other hand, all food has vanished from Middleton's table and the servants have left the room. Only wines, the catalysts of merriment, remain with the party. Everything from the cropped edges of the composition to the informal placement of figures speaks of the spirit and vivacity that Hamilton described as characteristic of Southerners. The gentlemen drawing a bow across a guitar case certainly bespeaks of gaiety.

134. Hamilton, 1:283–284. A like-minded opinion about the contrasting personalities of affluent Southerners and Northerners and its bearing on hospitality appears in Frederick Law Olmsted, *The Cotton Kingdom: . . .* (1953), p. 618 and pp. 614–622 *passim*; also, a similar view—"Much has been said in praise of the hospitality of the Southern planter, but they alone who have travelled in the Southern States, can appreciate the perfect ease and politeness with which a stranger is made to feel himself at home. . . . There is a warm and generous openess of character in the Southerners, which mere wealth and a retinue of servants cannot give; and they have often a dignity of manner, without stiffness, which is most agreeable"—is expressed by Lyell, 1:329.

135. Jane C. Nylander, "Henry Sargent's *Dinner Party* and *Tea Party*," in *Antiques, 121*, 5 (May 1982), p. 1176.

136. Carolina Art Association, *Selections From the Collection of the Carolina Art Association* (1977), p. 55.

Fig. 18. Henry Sargent, *The Dinner Party* (Boston, *ca.* 1821). (Courtesy of the Museum of Fine Arts, Boston; gift of Mrs. Horatio A. Lamb in memory of Mr. and Mrs. Winthrop Sargent.)

FIG. 19. Thomas Middleton, *Friends and Amateurs in Musick* (Charleston, *ca.* 1827). (Courtesy of the Carolina Art Association, Gibbes Art Gallery, Charleston.)

Judging from Middleton's furniture, he did not go to any great pains in pursuit of fashion. While the classical sideboard, pedestal table, and fancy chairs with rush seats were up-to-date, the elliptical end of a dining table and the knife box belonged to an earlier period and were out of fashion by 1827. Finally, the appreciation of art exampled by the music making and paintings shown in *Friends and Amateurs in Musick* reinforce the description of Southerners as high-minded. In contrast to Sargent's emphasis on family portraits and small landscapes and marines, Middleton's room is filled with paintings of subjects drawn from the higher plane of history, mythology, and religion.

V. Conduct of a Dinner

Being more dependent on social intercourse, they [Southerners] are at greater pains perhaps to render it agreeable.
Thomas Hamilton, 1833

JEREMIAH EVARTS, the New England lawyer and publisher, visited Savannah in 1822 as a convalescent.[137] He reluctantly accepted a dinner invitation on the assurance that "it should be a plain dinner without company and without ceremony."[138] After the meal Evarts commented in amazement, "Yet this was a dinner made for invalids: the luxury of this city, as exhibited at dinners, is very great."[139] Luckily his fairly complete account of the dinner has survived and can be taken as a typical upper-class dining experience in Savannah in 1822.

Before the guests arrived, the domestics set out the dining table, sideboard, and serving tables. Situating the dining table in the room and covering it with a green baize cloth were the first tasks. Then the damask cloth was symmetrically positioned over the green baize cloth. Next a servant arranged the napkins, water bottles, place settings, and silver serving pieces—fish knife, ladles, carving knives and forks, and tablespoons. Glasses for wine and dessert went on the sideboard in a semicircle. In addition, the sideboard furnished ample space for a stylish array of cruet stands,

137. Jeremiah Evarts, Diary, Saturday, March 30, 1822 (Manuscript Collection 240, Georgia Historical Society).

138. *Ibid.* Dinner invitations could be politely declined only if the refusal was grounded on a very strong and unavoidable cause. See William Kitchiner, *The Cook's Oracle: Containing Receipts for Plain Cookery on the Most Economic Plan for Private Families . . .* (1822), p. 41. Once set, dinner engagements were regarded as particularly binding, and guests were expected to be strictly punctual. See [Eliza Ware (Rotch) Farrar], *The Young Lady's Friend by a Lady* (1837), p. 341. The usual dinner hour was 2:00 or 3:00 P.M.

139. *Ibid.*

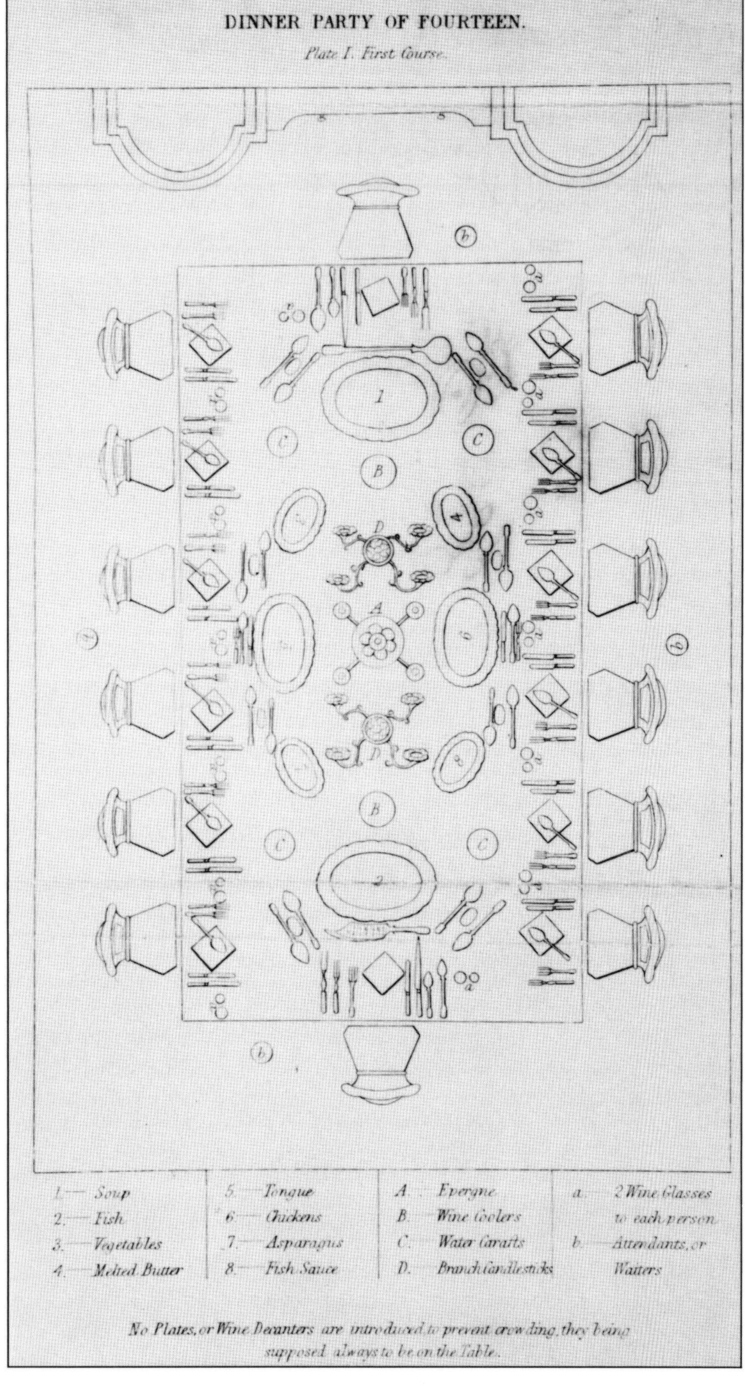

decanter stands, dessert wines, and small trays. It was customary to place dessert and salad plates as well as extra cutlery on the side table. Plates for each course and plate baskets for their removal also stood in readiness.[140]

Servants positioned the first course on the dining table before announcing dinner to the company assembled in the drawing room (fig. 20). Most dishes remained covered until the fish and/or soup were removed. In addition to fish and soup, the first course could include various roasted and boiled meats as well as a number of vegetables. On the day that Jeremiah Evarts was his guest, Dr. Kollock served a first course of "best dumb fish, with appropriate dressings, ducks, and southern bacon, oysters cooked in two ways, Irish potatoes in two ways, beets, onions, bread and boiled rice."[141]

In *A New System of Domestic Cookery*, Mrs. Rundell included a recipe "to dress Salt Cod, called Dumb Fish."[142] She instructed:

> Soak and clean the piece you mean to dress, then lay it all night in water, with a glass of vinegar. Boil it enough, then break it into flakes on the dish; pour over it parsnips boiled, beaten in a mortar, and then boil up with cream and a large piece of butter rubbed with a bit of flour. *The most usual way.* And perhaps the best, is to serve it up whole . . . with plenty of rich egg sauce.[143]

140. James Williams, *The Footman's Guide* [no date]; pp. 102–112.
141. Evarts, March 30, 1822.
142. [Mrs. Maria Eliza Rundell], *A New System of Domestic Cookery*, . . . (1817), p. 36.
143. *Ibid.*, pp. 36–37.

FIG. 20. "Dinner Party of Fourteen. Plate I. First Course," from James Williams, *The Footman's Guide* (London, n.d.). (Courtesy of the Research Libraries, the New York Public Library.)

Cod prepared in this way was very possibly what appeared on Dr. Kollock's table together with foods more characteristic of coastal Georgia, such as the ducks, bacon, oysters, and rice. Perhaps Dr. Kollock served the cod in hopes of pleasing his New England guest. If so, the gesture went unnoticed, for Evarts noted in his diary "I took duck, bacon, oysters, etc."[144]

Carving devolved to host, hostess, and guest alike. Mrs. Parkes recommended that "every lady should be able, when occasion calls for it, to carve without awkwardness, and should know what are considered the delicate parts of every dish that comes before her, that she may be able to point them out to others."[145] Servants held plates for carvers and served vegetables, sauces, and drinks. During the first course, guests might be offered water, porter, and ginger beer as well as light wines. Company often drank champagne between courses. After dinner the host proffered cordials, in addition to claret and Madeira. It was not obligatory for diners to partake of every dish. In fact Mrs. Farrar advised young ladies that "by dining on one dish, and that the plainest on the table, you will preserve your habitual temperance, and have time enough to be sociable with your neighbors."[146]

At the signal of the host the servants systematically removed the first course, beginning at the bottom of the table

144. Evarts, March 30, 1822.
145. Frances B. Parkes, *Domestic Duties* (1829), p. 69.
146. Farrar, p. 346.

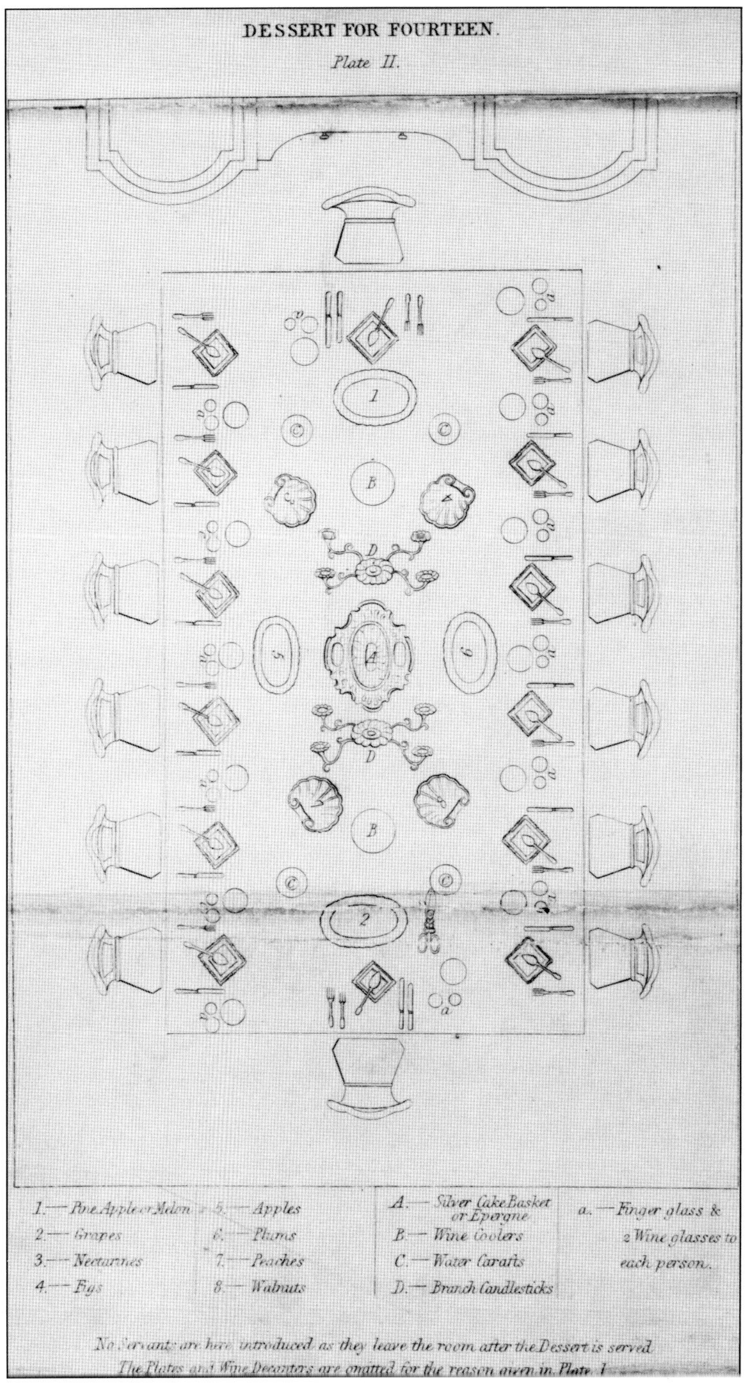

FIG. 21. "Dessert for Fourteen. Plate II," from James Williams, *The Footman's Guide* (London, n.d.). (Courtesy of the Research Libraries, the New York Public Library.)

and continuing to the left, to the top, and to the right.[147] The second course was served to the table in the same order. Appropriate dishes for a second course often included some entrées as well as cheesecakes, pies, puddings, stewed fruit, jellies, preserves, syllabubs, and other sweet dishes. Pies and puddings were everyday fare for family meals, while jellies and syllabubs were prepared for guests.

During a visit to Savannah, Mrs. Hillhouse of Washington, Georgia, wrote to her son. Her bemused description of the pretentious manners displayed in Savannah society is an excellent complement to the straightforward documentation of Evarts' diary. At the table where Mrs. Hillhouse was a guest, the entire second course was composed of a salad that "was dressed with all the airs and graces, displays of fingers, languishment of eyes, bows and simpers, etc. etc., by the fair hand of Mrs. M——, mother-in-law of [the host], who was dressed in the extreme fashion, (as a turban without border etc.) a widow belle of 60 odd years standing."[148]

Jeremiah Evarts recalled the second course at Dr. Kollock's table as comprising "cherry-pye, cranberry-pye, quince, orange and other preserves, with sallad, cheese, butter, and cream (beat to a foam with a flavor from juice of pineapple)."[149] From the second course Evarts selected the pineapple cream and cherry pie that he tasted "merely to judge the preservation of the cherries."[150] Offering guidance to the young, Mrs. Farrar suggested a rule of thumb: "If you are puzzled what to choose of all the variety which the second course presents, and the lady of the house invites you particularly to take of a certain dish, let that determine you."[151]

As the guests ate their puddings and pies, servants readied cheese plates, salad plates, and silverware. Keeping just ahead of the company, servants prepared dessert plates, glasses, and wines until the cheese was finished. Then the servants removed everything from the cloth, including crumbs, and put around the finger glasses. Variously called basins, dips, or cups, finger glasses appear regularly in Savannah inventories.[152] Yet they must have been unfamiliar to many Americans, because Mrs. Farrar felt it necessary to save her readers from mortification by forewarning that "if little glass bowls, with water in them, called finger-glasses, are served round to each person, at the end of the second course, it is that you may dip your fingers in and wipe them on your napkin."[153]

Mrs. Hillhouse scoffed at the affectations of her host in her narrative of the finger glasses: "Glass wash bowls were placed before each guest. The ablution was begun by Mrs. C—— washing her hands; Mr. C—— next washed face and hands, with many a hardy scrubbing. We followed as far as to wet our fingers and wipe them on napkins put on each plate."[154]

After taking away the finger glasses, a servant neatly removed the baize and damask tablecloths, rubbed the table,

147. Williams, pp. 119–120.
148. Boggs, p. 50.
149. Evarts, March 30, 1822.
150. *Ibid.*

151. Farrar, p. 347.
152. Inventories of Edward Telfair (1808), Barack Gibbons (1814), John Gibbons (1816), George Haig (1816), Philip Brosch (1825), Joseph Habersham (1832), William Gaston (1837), Priscilla Houstoun (1837), John Williamson (1843), and Henry McAlpin (1851).
153. Farrar, pp. 347–348.
154. Boggs, p. 50.

and brought on the dessert and wines (fig. 21). Mrs. Parkes commented that when the season allowed ripe fruit to be served as dessert "the most important, such as grapes, pineapples, peaches or apricots, must of course occupy the ends of the table; while the inferior fruits, such as strawberries and raspberries, with preserves and dried fruits, fill the corners and sides of the table."[155] Oranges and plantains, most likely from the West Indies, composed the fresh fruit at Dr. Kollock's table. Raisins and walnuts with several sorts of cordials and wines rounded out the dessert.

When the hostess beckoned, the ladies withdrew to the parlor, leaving the gentlemen who were, according to James Fenimore Cooper, "in the habit of sitting an hour or two after the cloth [was] removed, picking nuts, drinking wine, chatting, yawning, and gazing about the apartment."[156] Southerners were known for serving excellent Madeiras. Their dining rooms were frequently the stages for scenes like the one Thomas Hamilton recorded:

> The ladies have no sooner risen from the table, than the business of winebibbing commences in good earnest. The servants still remain in the apartment, and supply fresh glasses to the guests as the successive bottles make their appearance. To each of these a history is attached, and the vintage, the date of importation etc., are all duly detailed; then come the criticisms of the company, and as each bottle produced contains wine of a different quality from its predecessor, there is no chance of the topic being exhausted. At length, having made the complete tour of the cellar, proceeding progressively from commoner wines to those of finest flavor, the party adjourns to the drawing-room, and after, coffee, each guest takes his departure without ceremony of any kind.[157]

Departing immediately after coffee was the only polite course of action, for as Mrs. Farrar put it, "A dinner, well performed by all the actors in it, is very fatiguing, and, as it generally occupies three hours or more, most persons are glad to go away when it is fairly done."[158]

155. Parkes, p. 64.
156. James Fenimore Cooper, quoted in Berry B. Tracy, *Federal Furniture and Decorative Arts at Boscobel* (1981), p. 62.
157. Hamilton, 1:121.
158. Farrar, p. 349.

Part Two

Dining Furniture and Accessories

A SELECTIVE CATALOG OF THE TELFAIR AND THE RICHARDSON-OWENS-THOMAS HOUSE COLLECTION

Part Two: Dining Furniture and Accessories:

A Selective Catalog of the Telfair and the Richardson-Owens-Thomas House Collection

Note to the Catalog

This catalog is concerned with objects related to dining in the collection of the Telfair Academy of Arts and Sciences, Inc., and its satellite museum of the decorative arts, the Richardson-Owens-Thomas House. Objects on view at the Telfair and the Richardson-Owens-Thomas House are indicated with an asterisk (*) and a plus (+), respectively. The entries are divided into three sections: furniture, silver and silver plate, and ceramics and glass. Within the sections, objects are arranged chronologically. All objects cataloged here are found in the collection of the Telfair Academy unless designated as Richardson-Owens-Thomas House Collection. When the object cataloged is one of several nearly identical objects, such as dining chairs or teaspoons, only one of the set is cataloged and shown in the photograph. A numeral in parentheses to the right of the title of the object designates the number of objects in the set. Where sets of diverse objects, such as silver flatware or china, are cataloged, a brief description and dimensions are given for selected items that appear in illustrations.

I. Furniture

TABLES

1a Partial Set of Dining Tables (center section). *Ca.* 1790, American (possibly Georgia). H. 28 3/4″ (73 cm.); w. 48″ (122 cm.); d. 20 3/8″ (51.8 cm.). Bequest of Mary Telfair, 1875.

1b+ Partial Set of Dining Tables (D-end). *Ca.* 1820, American. H. 28 15/16″ (73.5 cm.); w. (open) 44 13/16″ (113.8 cm.); d. 47 3/4″ (121.2 cm.). Gift of Mrs. Eckley Coxe, 1954. Richardson-Owens-Thomas House Collection.

I am scored on all occasions for a set of dining tables, and to save my life have agreed to procure them. I will give you a description and beg of you to take the trouble to go to some of the best of your cabinet workmen and ascertain what they will cost, and to let me know as soon as a pigeon can fly from you to me. There must be a square table (all mahogany) with 8 legs with falling leaves. Two semi-circular ends fitted to the square table with six legs each, and a falling leaf to each, at the side of them, which is joined to the square table. We can then have a square, a circle, an oval, a parallelogram, or an oval parallelogram fit for from two to 20 persons to dine. It must all be made in the best manner of the best mahogany—it must be firm and lasting. And if the workmen should please us in quality and price we will employ him to make all our furniture. The money will be paid on delivery. We can procure them at Washington [Georgia] but concluded they will come hire and they may not be as good.[1]

1a

1b

Included in the plea of Thomas Fitch, the beleaguered husband in Milledgeville to his friend in Savannah, are several telling details evidencing the well-deserved and longstanding appeal of "sets of dining tables."

Fitch's description makes it easy to visualize their versatility. Equipped with castors, sets of dining tables could be rearranged and stored easily by lowering leaves or by placing sections against the wall. No gathering—from the large, formal dinner party to the intimate family meal—posed a seating problem to the owner of a set of dining tables. Imminently practical, individual sections of these tables often functioned as side tables in the dining room or elsewhere. Fitch described an elaborate, deluxe table with a total of twenty legs.[2] However, smaller three-part tables supported by twelve legs were more common. That a rural housewife clamored for a set of tables as her first major furniture acquisition is indicative of the central part these tables played in housekeeping. Reinforcing this idea is the very fact of their availability in rural Georgia and their frequent appearance in estate inventories of Savannahians through the 1850's.

Because the components of sets of dining tables stood on their own so well, they were all too easily divided up among heirs and others so that it is not unusual to find partial sets, such as those in the Telfair collection.

1. Thomas Fitch letter to Daniel Mulford, March 30, 1810 (Manuscript Collection 579, Georgia Historical Society).

2. Such a table (attributed to Duncan Phyfe's workshop) is found in the Boscobel Collection. See Berry B. Tracy, *Federal Furniture and Decorative Arts at Boscobel* (1981), pp. 68–69.

2. Dining table (fully extended)

2. Dining table (closed)

2+ Dining Table (accordion fold with eight leaves). *Ca.* 1815–1820, American (Philadelphia). Mahogany, brass inlay. Table: l. 50″ (127 cm.); w. 51 1/2″ (130.8 cm); h. 28 7/8″ (73.3 cm.). Leaves: w. 24 3/16″ (61.4 cm.); w. 23″ (58.4 cm.); w. 24 3/16″ (61.4 cm.); w. 23 1/4″ (59 cm.). Gift of Mrs. George Lorimer, 1958. Richardson-Owens-Thomas House Collection.

A distinct room reserved for dining was customary in the homes of wealthy Americans by the waning years of the eighteenth century.[3] In earlier times the main public rooms of a household served sundry purposes. Sets of dining tables were useful in multipurpose rooms. The table that comfortably seated twenty diners also could be separated into sections and inconspicuously stashed against the walls in order to transform the space into a sitting room. As the parlor was less and less called upon to do double duty, the dining table became a stationary focus of the specialized dining room.

Whereas it was no longer a great advantage to be able to break a large table down into small components, it was still necessary to accommodate parties of widely varying numbers. Invented around 1800, extension tables met this need with complicated mechanical contrivances that characterized the best work of the classical period.[4] An ingenious plan for an accordion fold substructure, shown in the London Society of Cabinet Makers price book for 1821 (fig. 22), was adapted in constructing this table. The frame telescopes to form a small table consisting of the two ends only and enlarges to accept as many as eight leaves.

Both the design and execution of this table suggest the hand of one of Philadelphia's preeminent artisans. Stylistic clues—overall quality of workmanship combined with carving in low relief as well as the use of reeding and rosettes—point simply to Philadelphia.[5] While a paucity of documented works makes attribution difficult, perhaps the most likely lead in seeking the authorship of the table is to be found with the firm of Joseph B. Barry and Son, which is known to have traded in Savannah.[6]

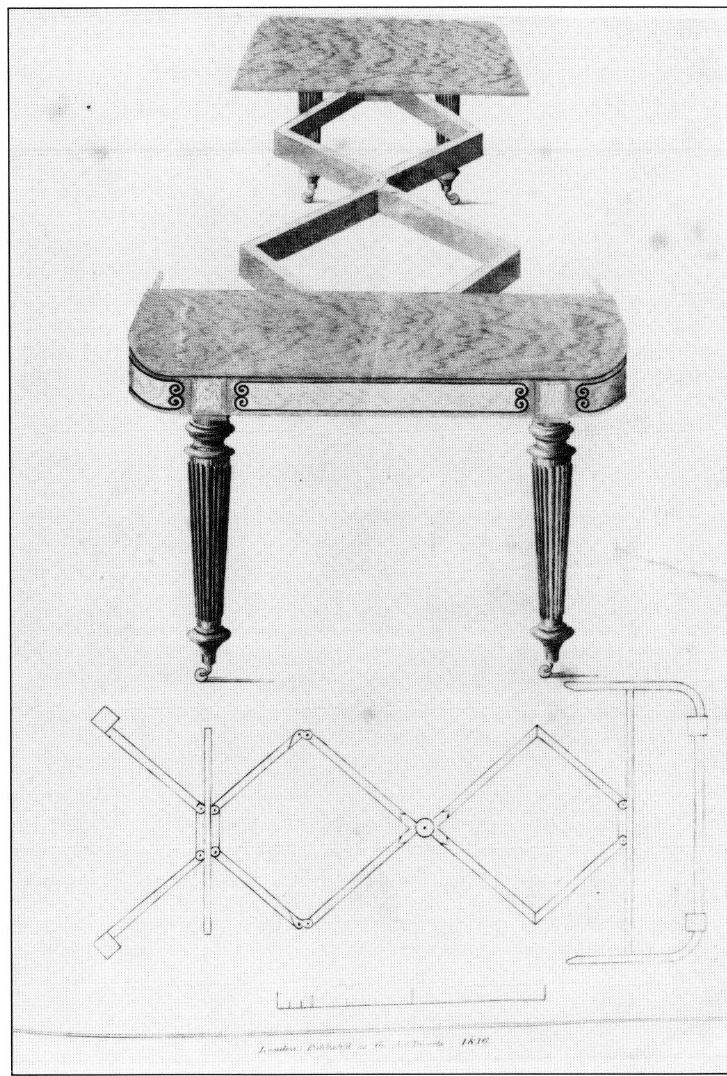

Fig. 22. Plate 5, from *The London Cabinet-makers Book of Prices, . . .* (London, 1821). (Courtesy of the Henry Francis du Pont Winterthur Museum Library: Collection of Printed Books and Periodicals.)

3. Old customs usually die slowly. As late as 1822, when an inventory was taken of the Richardson-Owens-Thomas House, a group of furnishings—including a set of dining tables, one marble slab or sideboard, twelve setting chairs, two armchairs, and one sofa—were found "in the Dining Room or Large Parlour," indicating an old-fashioned, multiple use of the room. See sale by Richard Richardson of furniture in his house, Oglethorpe Square, October 5, 1822, recorded April 7, 1823 (Chatham County Record of Deeds, *Deed Book 2M, 1822–1824*, pp. 43–44).

4. The Metropolitan Museum of Art, *Nineteenth-Century America: Furniture and Other Decorative Arts* (1970), catalog number 19. "One extension dinner table" appears in the inventory of John Williamson (1843). Otherwise, dining tables are undifferentiated as to form or described as sets in the inventories that were included in the survey.

5. Morrison H. Heckscher, "The Organization and Practice of Philadelphia Cabinetmaking Establishments, 1790–1820" (Master's thesis, University of Delaware, 1964), p. 78.

6. Katharine Wood Gross, "The Sources of Furniture Sold in Savannah, 1789–1815" (Master's thesis, University of Delaware, 1964), pp. 67–72.

3+ Pier or Side Table. *Ca.* 1815–1825, American (New York). Rosewood, marble top, stenciled gilt decoration. H. 38" (96.3 cm); w. 50" (27 cm.); d. 22 1/4" (56.5 cm.). Bequest of Miss Margaret Thomas, 1951. Richardson-Owens-Thomas House Collection.

The side or pier table in the dining room played a supporting role to the sideboard. It was set out similarly—that is, to create an elegant display with the "plates used at dinner, also the vegetables and cold meat, silver spoons, knives, and forks."[7] In addition, the side table served as a staging ground for the finger glasses.

Both handsome and functional, this pier table fits well into the fashionable dining room. Exhibiting very fine craftsmanship in elements such as the fully carved Ionic columns, this piece also achieved refinement in the mirrored back plate and stenciling. The

3

4

marble top was both stylish and functional as it could withstand the inevitable spills.

7. *The Domestic's Companion* (1834), p. 25.

4* Dining Table. Thomas Cook (active in Philadelphia 1828–1837). 1836, American (Philadelphia). Mahogany. H. 28 5/16" (71.5 cm.); diam. (no leaves) 52 1/2" (133.3 cm.); diam. (with small leaves) 72 1/2" (189.1 cm.); diam. (with large leaves) 85 1/2" (216.2 cm.). Bequest of Mary Telfair, 1875.

In 1836 Margaret Telfair purchased this circular dining table from Thomas Cook, the Philadelphia cabinetmaker.[8] Whereas rectangular dining tables were standard fare, the craftsman, such as Thomas Cook, who was aiming to build a circular table found no lack of design sources. For the Telfair table Cook adopted elements shown in pattern books by two different Englishmen. A fanciful forerunner of the "lazy susan" (fig. 23) offered by Thomas Sheraton in his *Designs for Household Furniture* (1812) inspired the general form for the eating surface of the table. Sheraton suggested a double top for the center section. The lower surface was fixed while the upper top was to be set on rollers so that diners might turn the dishes to any point they pleased.[9] Cook did not attempt the rollers, but he did equip his table with removable outer leaves like the ones Sheraton had shown. In fact Cook improved on Sheraton by fitting out the Telfair table with two different-sized sets of semicircular leaves in an attempt to approach the versatility of rectangular tables. Wisely eschewing what would have been an extremely unwieldy tilt-top, Cook took only the design for the support of the Telfair table from Richard Brown (fig. 24).

8. Probably ordered during the Telfairs' annual visit to the North, the table was ready for shipment at the time of the first frost, just before they sailed for Savannah. Mary Telfair sent the following receipt and message

Fig. 23. New design for a dining table, plate 31, from T[homas] Sheraton, *Designs for Household Furniture* . . . (London, 1812). (Courtesy of the Henry Francis du Pont Winterthur Museum Library: Collection of Printed Books and Periodicals.)

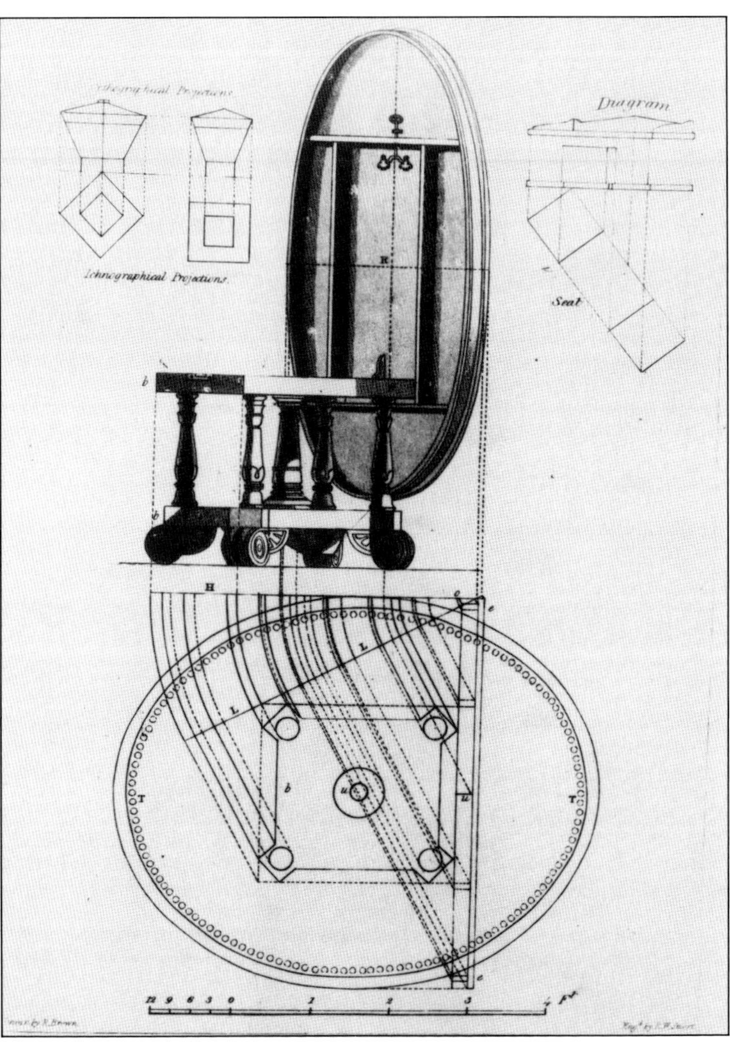

Fig. 24. A dining-table, plate 11, from Richard Brown, *The Rudiments of Drawing Cabinet and Upholstery Furniture* (London, 1822). (Courtesy of the Henry Francis du Pont Winterthur Museum Library: Collection of Printed Books and Periodicals.)

from Philadelphia to her sister Margaret in New York: "Rec[d] Oct 25th 1836 of Miss Telfair/One hundred dollars in full for circular/Dining Table—For Thos. Cook/$100 J[no] G. Franklin/Just as I had dispatched my last epistle my dear Margaret—the above named Franklin bowed himself into our presence with Bill of Lading . . . in one hand, and a receipt in the other—I seated his Honor, gave him this sheet of paper, and dispatch[ed] his autograph, paid him your money, talked of Armoures to him and wished him good morning" (Mary Telfair letter to Margaret Telfair, October 25, 1836 [Manuscript Collection 793, Georgia Historical Society]).

9. Thomas Sheraton, *Cabinet Encyclopedia* (London, 1804–1807), pp. 7–8.

SIDEBOARDS

5 Sideboard. *Ca.* 1795–1805, American (New York). Mahogany, light wood inlay. H. 39 3/4" (100.9 cm.); w. 72" (182.8 cm.); d. 31" (78.7 cm.). Bequest of Mary Telfair, 1875.

5

During America's post-Revolutionary period, fashionable dining evolved as a lavish ritual with a new furniture form, the sideboard, as its emblem. By the 1820's American servants' manuals, largely based on English prototypes, codified the conduct of the dinner party. The sideboard is the altar to conspicuous consumption in Robert Robert's precise instructions to servants preparing for the ceremonial rite of ostentatious dining:

> In setting out your sideboard, you must study neatness, convenience, and taste; as you must think that ladies and gentlemen that have splendid and costly articles, wish to have them seen and set out to the best advantage. . . . Sideboards . . . set out in proper order . . . make a magnificent appearance. There are some old and experienced servants, that will set out their tables and sideboards with such a degree of taste and neatness, that they will strike the eyes of every person who enters the room, with a pleasing sensation of elegance.[10]

Roberts advised that the dessert grapes and all the spare glasses must go on the sideboard, with the champagne, hock, and ale glasses. He continued: "When all these are properly arranged, they make a grand display. Your glasses should form a crescent, or half circle, as this looks most sublime. . . . In the space between the glasses,"[11] at the center of the sideboard, one placed the cruet stand or casters. They were flanked by the two water decanters and the small, silver hand waiters—one on each side of each water decanter—then the wine for the dessert, in the silver coasters. Any vacancy was filled with spoons, "as spoons, etc. give glass a brilliant display."[12] No wonder Americans from North to South looked on the sideboards as an essential of dining paraphernalia.

This Telfair sideboard originated in New York, perhaps in the shop of William Whitehead.[13] It is identical in its distinctive forms to two documented Whitehead sideboards.[14] In each instance there is a large case, both wide and deep, distinguished by cupboard doors and drawers with ornamental convex and sweeping serpentine curves. The cases are raised on six thin, tapering legs. Because Whitehead may have been involved in a partnership pursuing the coastwise trade, it is possible that a member of the Telfair family purchased the sideboard from a sea captain on the docks.[15] In fact there were numerous furniture items in Edward Telfair's countinghouse on the wharf at the time of his death in 1807.[16] However, it is just as likely to have been purchased by a Telfair during the course of an annual visit to the North.

10. Robert Roberts, *The House Servant's Directory* (1977), pp. 48–49.
11. *Ibid.*, p. 49.
12. *Ibid.*, pp. 49–50.
13. Regrettably, crude workmanship possibly attributable to a poorly executed and all but undocumented restoration make it impossible to assign the work to Whitehead, whose other known works are highly refined.
14. Wendy A. Cooper, *In Praise of America* (1980), p. 22.
15. *Ibid.*, p. 267.
16. Inventory of Edward Telfair (1808).

6

6+ Sideboard. *Ca.* 1810–1815. American (Boston). Mahogany, gilt brass pulls. H. 42 1/4″ (107.3 cm.); w. 80 3/8″ (204.1 cm.); 27″ (68.5 cm.). Gift of Mr. and Mrs. Franklin R. Dulany, 1965.

In spite of its relatively recent introduction, the sideboard was well grounded in the everyday life of Savannah's upper class by the first quarter of the nineteenth century. Generally the sideboard was the most valuable household possession. Further, a mahogany sideboard was the single most expensive furniture item discovered in a sampling of upper-class inventories. The highest-valued sideboard belonged to Thomas Telfair (1786–1818) and was appraised at $200 in his estate inventory.[17]

While it is not historically connected with Savannah, this sideboard is a good example of the costly materials and skilled workmanship that went into manufacturing high style furniture. Several discreetly distinctive elements are combined in this piece to produce a richly harmonious whole. The manipulation of the wood is masterful throughout, from the posts carved with rosettes near the top and acanthus leaves at the knees to the choice of richly marked mahogany veneers and the effective use of moldings to enclose and highlight the veneers. Finally, the proportional relationships of the case to legs and bowed center section to the flanking cupboards are all carried out with perfect ease and taste. Similarities of this piece to other acknowledged works suggests the authorship of the Thomas Seymour firm of Boston.[18]

17. Inventory of Thomas Telfair (1818). The sideboard valued at $200 is undoubtedly the same piece specified in Thomas Telfair's will, dated March 2, 1818: "*Item* I give my new sideboard to my sister Sarah Haig" (will of Thomas Telfair [1818]). The second and third most costly sideboards were

appraised at $80 and $70, with others ranging from $5 to $60. (Inventories of George Haig [1816] and Isaiah Davenport [1828]).

18. Vernon C. Stoneman, *John and Thomas Seymour, Cabinetmakers in Boston, 1794–1816* (1959), p. 157; and *Supplement* . . . (1965), p. 38.

7* Sideboard. Attributed to Duncan Phyfe (1768–1854). *Ca.* 1815, American (New York). Mahogany. H. 56″ (142.2 cm.); w. 78″ (198 cm.); d. 24 1/2″ (62.2 cm.). Bequest of Mary Telfair, 1875.

Monumental in its presence, yet precisely crafted in every detail, this sideboard is a powerful example of the artistry of Duncan Phyfe. Paralleling the tendency of Regency architects to allow broad facades to stand alone, uncomplicated by applied decoration, Phyfe chose a rich, flame-grained mahogany for the case of the sideboard. Simply stated columns and pilasters continue the architectonic metaphor and echo the decorative vocabulary of the Regency taste.

While the overall effect is grandiose, Phyfe's trademarks of attention to detail and careful craftsmanship are clearly present in this sideboard. They are apparent in the ormolu capitals as well as the fine fluting and brass inlay on the inverted pilasters. The craftsman's sensitivities to the functions of the sideboard—both practical and ceremonial—are clearly spelled out in details, such as the cabinets fitted out for adjustable shelves and the mirrored splashboard that redoubles the dazzling visual effect of glass and plate set out for a dinner party.

Distinguished in both business and craft, Phyfe established a clientele that extended well beyond New York and into the provinces. Whereas members of the Gibbons-Telfair family placed orders with Phyfe in New York, it was also possible to buy Phyfe's furniture through J. W. Morrell, his agent in Savannah.[19] In July 1802 William Gibbons went on a buying spree in New York,

7

where he purchased a pair of card tables and a tea table from Phyfe.[20] Later, roughly between 1808 and 1818, Mary Telfair also patronized Phyfe's shop. She ordered both a secretary and a worktable.[21] Out of these five items only the whereabouts of the secretary are known today. On the other hand, we have in the sideboard a Phyfe work that descended in the Telfair family without a paper trail to substantiate its origin. Thomas Telfair's will, however, may give a clue in "*Item* I give my new sideboard to my sister Sarah Haig."[22]

19. "*Mahogany and Easy Chairs* and Hair Mattresses just received from . . . New York, an assortment of Mahogany and Easy Chairs, Hair Mattresses, Card Tables, Tea Tables, Sofa, etc. etc. All of the latest fashions, which will be sold low on application to J. W. Morrell agent for D. Phyfe, New York, Church Buildings opposite Gibbons Buildings" (*The Georgian and Evening Advertiser* [May 2, 1821], p. 4).

20. Account book of William Gibbons, January 12, 1802–April 4, 1804 (Manuscript Collection 793, Georgia Historical Society).

21. Mary Telfair's patronage of Phyfe came to light in her correspondence with Mary Few, her lifelong friend. In one letter Mary Telfair inquired: "Have you paid Phyfe a visit & what does he say about the Secretary?—. . . PS Keep the change of the hundred after you settle with Phyfe [   ] and pay for the blank book as I may trouble you soon if you have no objection to being my Banker" (Mary Telfair letter to Mary Few, October 28, [1816], William Few Papers, Georgia Department of Archives and History). In another letter Mary Telfair writes: "Thank you for the Pelice which arrived in safety but I must trouble you dear Mary to call on Phyfe; you recollect I paid him sixty dollars for my work Table & $1 50 cts for boxing it, he never sent it on board the Tybee as he promised and probably if any accident happened to the Table he will be honest enough to return you the money" (Mary Telfair letter to Mary Few, December 8, [*ca.* 1809–1818], William Few Papers, Georgia Department of Archives and History).

22. Will and inventory of Thomas Telfair (1818).

CHAIRS

8 Side Chair (4). *Ca.* 1802, American (New York). Painted wood, rush bottom. H. 37 7/8" (83.6 cm.); w. 18 1/8" (46.1 cm.); d. 16" (40.7 cm.). Bequest of Mary Telfair, 1875.

8

Dozens upon dozens of painted, otherwise called fancy, chairs appeared in Savannah inventories between 1800 and 1855. Versatile and reasonably priced, they were used in both drawing and dining rooms. William Gibbons owned four dozen fancy chairs at the time of his death in 1804. Two dozen were variously described as red or yellow and green while there were one dozen each of white and gilt and black and yellow.[23]

These four black and yellow fancy chairs were probably once part of the set of twelve owned by William Gibbons. Certain stylistic elements—such as the liberal use of gilt balls, scroll backs, bell-shaped seats, and out-flaring front feet—suggest a New York origin of the chairs. And, in fact, William Gibbons' accounts for his New York trip made in July 1802 confirm that he paid "Joseph Riley for 12 chairs at 1.62 1/4 = 19.50."[24] His will stipulates: "Item. I give and bequeath unto my sister *Sarah Telfair* . . . One doz. chairs painted black and yellow."[25] Entered in his estate inventory are "1 doz chairs painted black and yellow" valued at "$18.50," only $1 less than what he paid Joseph Riley for chairs two years earlier.

An extraordinarily informative sequence of documents, such as those relating to the accounts and estate of William Gibbons, are valuable not only because of the light they shed on Gibbons, but also because they add bit by bit to the biographies of specific craftsmen such as Riley and generally to a growing body of knowledge about American retailing.

23. Inventory of William Gibbons (1804).
24. Account book of William Gibbons, 1802–1804.
25. Will of William Gibbons (1803).

9

9 Armchair.[26] *Ca.* 1802, American (New York). Painted wood, rush seat. H. 33 1/4" (84.5 cm.); 18 1/16" (45.9 cm.); d. 16 1/8" (41 cm.). Bequest of Mary Telfair, 1875.

Fancy chairs, particularly at the time of their introduction, belonged to the pantheon of high style. Later, affordability contributed greatly to their attaining ubiquity in the American home. This chair has much to recommend it to the ranks of the high style fancy chair. The slender, elegant members are turned in imitation of bamboo. Both arms and back are very gracefully curved to accommodate the human form during a long dinner. The seat is broad and comfortable. Even though the chair is in poor condition, some of the original decoration remains. Paint analysis indicates that the initial finish was white and gilt.

The origins of this handsome chair are uncertain. However, as with many objects that descended in the Gibbons-Telfair family, the records of William Gibbons may give a clue. He entered in his account book: "Paid Palmer for one dozen bamboo gilt chairs at 3.50 each and 4.50 for 2 armed each—44.00."[27] This merchant is most certainly the same Palmer who ran an ad in the New York *Republican Watch-Tower* on February 27, 1802, as follows:

> WILLIAM PALMER.—Fancy Chairs & Cornices. William Palmer, No. 3 Nassau-street, near the Federal-hall, has for sale a large assortment of elegant, well made, and highly finished black and gold, &c. Fancy Chairs, with cane and rush bottoms. . . .
>
> Old chairs re-painted, regilt, &c. at the lowest price, and agreeable to any pattern. Ornamented painting and gilding neatly executed. N. B. Orders from any part of the Continent will be gratefully received, and punctually executed.[28]

The progress of the chairs can be picked up again in Gibbons' will when he writes: "Item. I give and bequeath unto my brother *Barack Gibbons* . . . 1 dozen chairs painted white and [gilt]"[29] and traced on to his estate inventory as "1 doz chairs painted white & gilt 32.50."[30]

26. This chair is the only known survivor of a set that probably originally comprised two armchairs and ten side chairs.
27. Account book of William Gibbons, 1802–1804.
28. Quoted in Rita Susswein Gottesman, *The Arts and Crafts in New York, 1800–1804* (1965), no. 361.
29. Will of William Gibbons (1803).
30. Inventory of William Gibbons (1804).

10

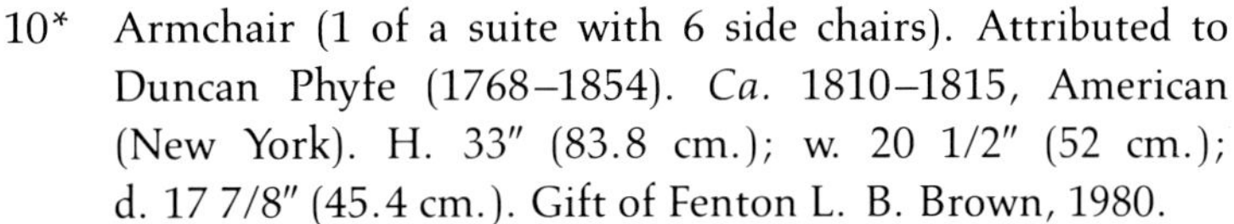

10* Armchair (1 of a suite with 6 side chairs). Attributed to Duncan Phyfe (1768–1854). *Ca.* 1810–1815, American (New York). H. 33" (83.8 cm.); w. 20 1/2" (52 cm.); d. 17 7/8" (45.4 cm.). Gift of Fenton L. B. Brown, 1980.

A purchaser ordering custom chairs from a craftsman in the early nineteenth century could select features from a range of options to suit his budget and taste. A prototype for this chair can be found under the heading of "A Scroll Back Chair" in the *New-York Revised Prices for Manufacturing Cabinet and Chair Work* for 1810. This armchair was one of the most elegant and expensive chairs a purchaser could order. The basic price for a scroll-back chair was £1.2.8 in 1810. This model, however, incorporates a number of "extras"—including bell seat, extra sweep from rails, scroll sweep elbows arms, an ogee splat instead of a straight one, and others, which would bring the price up to £2.10.1.[31]

31. Wendy A. Cooper, *In Praise of America* (1980), p. 252.

11+ Side Chair (12). *Ca.* 1815, American (Philadelphia). Mahogany, dark wood inlay. H. 33 1/2" (85.1 cm.); w. 19" (48.1 cm.); d. 17 7/8" (45.3 cm.). Gift of Miss Maude Bryan Foote, 1959 and 1971. Gift of Mr. and Mrs. Everette E. Ellis, 1961. Gift of Mary Letitia Spraul in memory of Miss Maude Bryan Foote, 1974. Richardson-Owens-Thomas House Collection.

11

The Grecian *klismos* chair was a very popular expression of the classical taste in the United States. Derived from chairs shown on ancient Greek vases, the basic profile included saber legs that swept into curving stiles, ornamental splats, and shaped and/or scroll-backs. In the hands of different craftsmen, regional and individual interpretations of the basic form flourished. Although it cannot be assigned to a specific maker, this chair betrays its Philadelphia origins in features such as the shallow carving, the use of moldings and rosettes, and the shaped crest rail.

Although mahogany chairs are normally associated with formal dining, they were far less common in the first half of the nineteenth century than one might imagine. In a sampling of documents from estates and sales, 1800–1855, only eight sets of mahogany dining chairs appeared.[32] Two belonged to members of the Telfair family, Edward and his son, Thomas. The property of Richard Richardson, original owner of the Richardson-Owens-Thomas House, included a third. Not only immensely popular, but also less expensive than their mahogany counterparts, painted or fancy chairs were far more typical even in upper-class homes.

32. Inventories of Joseph Clay (1805), Edward Telfair (1808), Joseph Bryan (1813), John Gibbons (1816), Thomas Telfair (1818), Joseph Stiles (1839), and John Williamson (1843); and the sale of Richard Richardson (1822). Most sets numbered twelve or fourteen chairs as opposed to the meager eight we are accustomed to today.

12

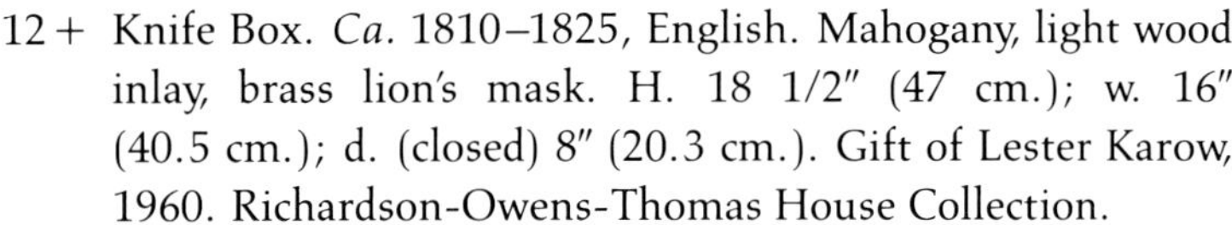

12+ Knife Box. *Ca.* 1810–1825, English. Mahogany, light wood inlay, brass lion's mask. H. 18 1/2" (47 cm.); w. 16" (40.5 cm.); d. (closed) 8" (20.3 cm.). Gift of Lester Karow, 1960. Richardson-Owens-Thomas House Collection.

A standard accessory found in the dining rooms of most upper-class homeowners, the knife box housed both forks and knives, but rarely spoons. Knife boxes are most frequently entered in Savannah inventories in pairs. They are also listed, however, singly and in threes. In addition to serving a practical purpose of providing storage for cutlery, knife boxes often formed part of the ornamental display on the sideboard. Ordinarily knife boxes were not purchased from the makers of sideboards. There are a few recorded instances, however, in which knife boxes were made as matching accessories for a particular sideboard.

This knife box is distinguished by an ingenious apparatus that is characteristic of much of the better workmanship of the early nineteenth century. While the typical knife case is fitted with a hinged top that is raised to reveal the interior of the box, this case has no lid. Here the semicircular storage compartment turns on a pivot. When closed, the flat side forms the face of the cabinet. When opened, the semicircular compartment extends beyond the cabinet, revealing the contents of the box.

II. Silver and Silver Plate

FLATWARE
Ladles

13a + Punch Ladle. Ebenezer Whiting (1735–1794). *Ca.* 1786–1788, American (Savannah). Silver. L. 13 7/16″ (34.2 cm.). Gift of Descombe Wells, 1961. Richardson-Owens-Thomas House Collection.

13b Punch Ladle. Arthur Rice (1785–1808) or Joseph Rice (1761–1807). *Ca.* 1800, American (Savannah). Silver. L. 13 5/8″ (34.5 cm.). Gift of James A. Williams, 1968.

13c Punch Ladle. Josiah Penfield (1785–1828). *Ca.* 1820, American (Savannah). Silver. L. 12 3/4″ (32.4 cm.). Gift of Thelma R. Rosen in memory of her husband, Dr. Emanuel F. Rosen, 1986.

13d Soup Ladle. Frederick Marquand (1799–1882). 1821, American (Savannah). Silver. L. 13 1/4″ (33.7 cm.). Gift of James A. Williams, 1968.

13e Soup Ladle. Frederick Marquand (1799–1882). 1822, American (Savannah). Silver. L. 13 1/4″ (33.7 cm.). Museum purchase, 1982.

13f + Sauce Ladle. Moses Eastman (1794–1850). *Ca.* 1830, American (Savannah). Silver. L. 7 3/4″ (17.7 cm.). Bequest of Miss Margaret Thomas, 1951. Richardson-Owens-Thomas House Collection.

13g + Sauce Ladle. Attributed to Samuel Wilmot (active 1825–1856). American (possibly Savannah). Silver. L. 7 3/16″ (18.3 cm.). Gift of Descombe Wells, 1961. Richardson-Owens-Thomas House Collection.

Front view, top to bottom: 13a, 13b, 13c

Back view, top to bottom: 13a, 13b, 13c

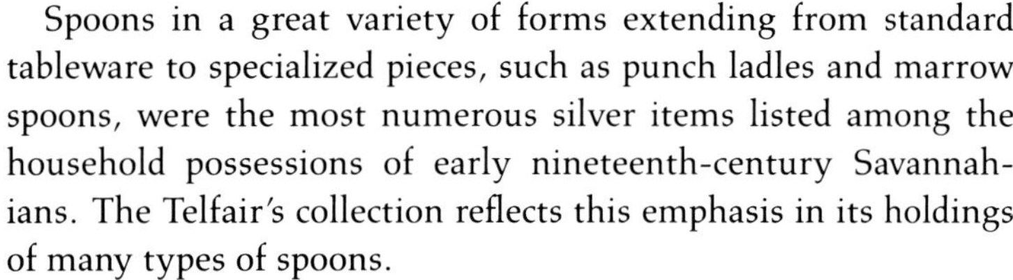

Spoons in a great variety of forms extending from standard tableware to specialized pieces, such as punch ladles and marrow spoons, were the most numerous silver items listed among the household possessions of early nineteenth-century Savannahians. The Telfair's collection reflects this emphasis in its holdings of many types of spoons.

Among the ladles in the Telfair collection are examples made by several of the principals of a long-lived and diversified firm of Savannah silversmiths. Isaac Marquand (1766–1838) founded the business in 1800. Marquand, who was to become even more distinguished as an entrepreneur than as a silversmith, jeweler, and watchmaker, soon took Cornelius Paulding of New York as a partner to form the firm of Marquand and Paulding.

Marquand's mercantile interests came to the fore early in his career. In the announcement of his partnership with Paulding, Marquand also advertised new goods just received from Europe and New York.[33] It was not unusual for silversmiths to sell other metalwares in addition to their own production. Marquand, however, offered for sale a wide variety of products, including paper hangings and bordering, looking glasses, china chimney pieces, and riding chairs. Watchmaking and silversmithing soon dwindled to a very small part of his business enterprises. In June 1803 he departed Savannah to make New York his headquarters while Paulding operated the business in Savannah.

Shortly after his arrival in Savannah, Marquand had taken his teenage nephew Josiah Penfield into the business, most likely as an apprentice.[34] The boy must have demonstrated an aptitude for the business and the craft, because Marquand and Paulding delegated much of the responsibility for the Savannah firm to him. In the meantime they occupied themselves with concerns in New York and New Orleans, respectively. In 1810 they rewarded the twenty-two-year-old Penfield with a partnership and renamed the Savannah firm Marquand, Paulding, and Penfield. Day-to-day business affairs must have occupied a great deal of Penfield's time. Nevertheless there are silver objects stamped with his mark (cat. 13c).

Front view, top to bottom: 13d, 13e

Back view, top to bottom: 13d, 13e

In 1815 Marquand and Paulding withdrew from the Savannah firm, leaving Penfield as the sole proprietor. Josiah Penfield operated as the successor to the original Marquand firm until 1820, when Marquand's son, Frederick, joined him in the formation of Josiah Penfield and Co. Frederick remained in Savannah until 1826. During his time in Savannah he created a variety of fine silver objects that have survived (cat. 13d, 13e). Among the smiths associated with the firm, Frederick is best represented in the Telfair collection.

After Frederick Marquand's departure for New York in 1826, Moses Eastman joined Josiah Penfield and Co., where he continued until Penfield's death in 1828. Moses Eastman carried on in the business under his own name until his death in 1850. Telfair owns a number of objects bearing his mark (cat. 13f).

Isaac Marquand was a skilled businessman who amassed an impressive fortune and passed on much of his business savvy to his sons. They in turn are still well remembered for their benefactions, such as the Marquand Pavilion of Bellevue Hospital, New York. Silversmiths connected with the Marquand firm enjoyed financial success and civic involvement that was fairly common among members of their trade. In fact the status of the silversmith in early American society was comparable to that of today's professional.

Likewise Marquand's successors in the Savannah firm, Penfield and Eastman, committed their resources to philanthropy. Penfield led an active life of public service, and his legacies benefited many charitable organizations. His bequests included $2,500 "to create a fund for the education of pious young men for the gospel ministry."[35] These monies provided the impetus to Mercer University, which was established at Penfield, Greene County, Georgia. Like his predecessor Penfield, Moses Eastman participated in many community activities. At the time of his death in 1850, Eastman was erecting a gothic church that he intended to present to the Unitarian congregation in Savannah. His widow completed the project.

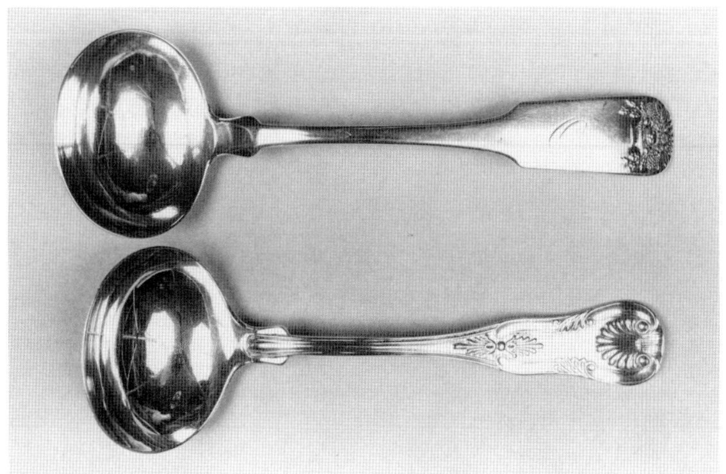

Front view, top to bottom: 13f, 13g

Back view, top to bottom: 13f, 13g

33. "Isaac Marquand, Watchmaker," in *The Columbian Museum and Savannah Advertiser* (January 1, 1802), p. 1; and "Isaac Marquand," in *The Columbian Museum and Savannah Advertiser* (January 15, 1802), p. 1.

34. Boys usually entered a seven-year apprenticeship at the age of fourteen.

35. George Barton Cutten, *The Silversmiths of Georgia, Together With Watchmakers and Jewelers, 1733 to 1850* (1958), p. 100.

Teaspoons, Tablespoons, and Dessert and Serving Spoons

14a Teaspoons (2). Arthur Rice (1785–1808). *Ca.* 1800, American (Savannah). Silver. L. 5 1/2" (14 cm.). Gift of James A. Williams, 1968. Richardson-Owens-Thomas House Collection.

14b Large Serving Spoon. Joseph Rice (1761–1807). *Ca.* 1800, American (Savannah). Silver. L. 15 7/16" (39.2 cm.).

14c + Teaspoons (6). Nathaniel Butler (1760–1829). *Ca.* 1800, American (possibly Savannah). Silver. L. 6" (15.2 cm.). Gift of Descombe Wells, 1961. Richardson-Owens-Thomas House Collection.

14d Teaspoons (4). John Pearson (active in Savannah 1802–1817). *Ca.* 1802, American (Savannah). Silver. L. 5 5/16" (13.5 cm.). Gift of Thelma R. Rosen in memory of her husband, Dr. Emanuel F. Rosen, 1986.

14e Tablespoons (3). John Pearson (active in Savannah 1802–1817). *Ca.* 1805, American (Savannah). Silver. L. 9 1/16" (23.0 cm.). Gift of Thelma R. Rosen in memory of her husband, Dr. Emanuel F. Rosen, 1986.

14f Dessert Spoon. John Ewan (1786–1852). *Ca.* 1810, American (Charleston). Silver. L. 6 7/8" (17.5 cm.). Gift of Mrs.

Leroy King, 1962. Richardson-Owens-Thomas House Collection.

14g Teaspoons (8). William Thomson (active in New York 1810–1833, 1841–1845). *Ca.* 1815, American (New York). Silver. L. 5 15/16″ (15.1 cm.). Bequest of Miss Margaret Thomas, 1951. Richardson-Owens-Thomas House Collection.

14h Teaspoons (4). Frederick Marquand (1799–1882). 1821, American (Savannah). Silver. L. 5 1/2″ (14 cm.). Gift of James A. Williams, 1968.

14i Dessert Spoons (2). Frederick Marquand (1799–1882). 1821, American (Savannah). Silver. L. 7 1/8″ (18.2 cm.). Gift of James A. Williams, 1968.

14j Teaspoons (2). Frederick Marquand (1799–1882). 1821, American (Savannah). Silver. L. 5 5/8″ (14.3 cm.). Gift of James A. Williams, 1968.

14k Teaspoons (3). David B. Nichols (1791–1860). *Ca.* 1825, American (Savannah). Silver. L. 5 11/16″ (14.5 cm.). Gift of the children of Mr. and Mrs. Malcolm Bell, Sr., 1969. Richardson-Owens-Thomas House Collection.

14l Teaspoons (3). Frederick Marquand (1799–1882). 1825, American (Savannah). Silver. L. 5 13/16″ (14.7 cm.). Gift of James A. Williams, 1968.

14m Teaspoons (3). Frederick Marquand (1799–1882). 1821, American (possibly Savannah). Silver.

14n Teaspoon. Moses Eastman (1798–1850). *Ca.* 1826–1830, American (Savannah). Silver. L. 5 3/4″ (14.6 cm.). Gift of Thelma R. Rosen in memory of her husband, Dr. Emanuel F. Rosen, 1986.

14o Dessert Spoon. Marquand and Co. (active in New York 1833–1839). *Ca.* 1835, American (New York). Silver. L. 7 1/16″ (17.9 cm.).

14p Pierced Serving Spoon. Thomas Wriggins (active in Philadelphia 1831–1867). *Ca.* 1840, American (Philadelphia). Silver. L. 8″ (20.3 cm.). Bequest of Gertrude West Hollowbush, 1988.

14q Dessert Spoon. Thomas T. Wilmot (active in Savannah 1843–1850). *Ca.* 1843–1850, American (Savannah). Silver. L. 8 5/8″ (21.9 cm.). Gift of Thelma R. Rosen in memory of her husband, Dr. Emanuel F. Rosen, 1986.

14r Dessert Spoon. Attributed to Joel N. Freeman (active in Augusta, Ga., *ca.* 1853–1860). *Ca.* 1855, American (Augusta). Silver. L. 8 7/8″ (21.4 cm.). Gift of Thelma R. Rosen in memory of her husband, Dr. Emanuel F. Rosen, 1986.

Prior to the second quarter of the nineteenth century, spoons were by far the silver objects most commonly found in the household and estate inventories of Savannahians. Like other cities of a similar size, Savannah had a full complement of smiths producing silver products.[36] A sampling of their spoons drawn from the Telfair collection illustrates many key elements of the classical style in American spoon design.

By 1800 spoons with rounded handles and bright-cut borders were no longer as fashionable as they had been in the 1780's and 1790's. Nevertheless the Irish-born Arthur Rice found a market for spoons with the slender, elegant shafts and restrained engraved decoration in the Savannah market (cat. 14a).

The canted corners of coffin handle spoons rose in popularity around 1800. Spoons such as those made by Nathaniel Butler retained the simplicity and delicacy of the Federal style in their tapering handles, feathered script monograms, and elongated oval bowls (cat. 14c).

After the turn of the nineteenth century, classicism took on a

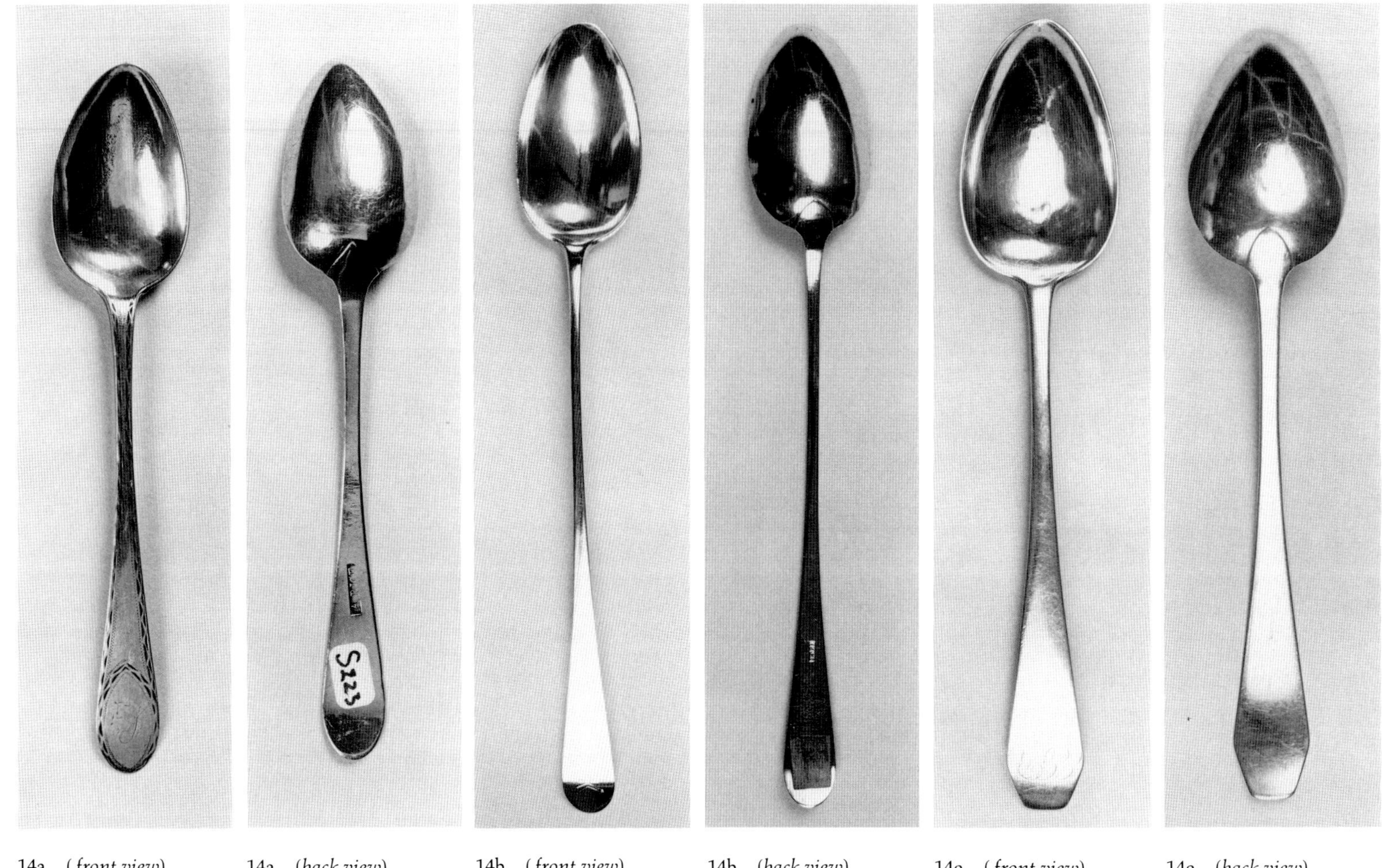

14a (*front view*) 14a (*back view*) 14b (*front view*) 14b (*back view*) 14e (*front view*) 14e (*back view*)

robustness uncharacteristic of Federal forms. A dessert spoon by John Ewan exhibits the emerging trend of 1810 in the fiddle handle, the flaring shoulders of the shaft, and the larger, more rounded bowl (cat. 14f). As the fiddle handle shape increased in popularity, silversmiths developed a number of decorative variations to the basic form, which also remained stylish for several decades. The most fundamental of these modifications was single or double ridging around the edge of the shaft. The fiddle-thread pattern is illustrated in a spoon made by Joel Freeman, around 1855 (cat. 14r).

Stamped embellishments of the simple fiddleback, such as the shell, basket of flowers, and sheaf of wheat patterns, gained prominence in the 1820's. Frederick Marquand employed the shell motif on the back of the bowl as well as on the handle of the spoon (cat. 14h). The basket of flowers and sheaf of wheat patterns, in particular, represent the vitality of the classicism of the American Empire style as well as a growing appreciation on the part of Americans of the rich bounty of their land. Specimens of these motifs are found in the work of Frederick Marquand, Moses Eastman, and Thomas T. Wilmot (cat. 14j, 14l, 14n, 14q).

36. Newspaper advertisements dating from the mid-eighteenth century forward verify that Savannah smiths made silver in a great variety of forms. Unfortunately relatively few of these pieces are known to us today. The fires of 1796 and 1820 as well as subsequent disasters have apparently taken their toll.

Front view, top to bottom: 14c, 14d, 14k, 14h, 14g

Back view, top to bottom: 14c, 14d, 14k, 14h, 14g

Front view, top to bottom: 14j, 14m, 14n, 14l

Back view, top to bottom: 14j, 14m, 14n, 14l

Front view, left to right: 14f, 14i, 14o

Back view, left to right: 14f, 14i, 14o

14p (*front view*) 14p (*back view*) 14q (*front view*) 14q (*back view*) 14r (*front view*) 14r (*back view*)

Sugar Tongs

15a + Sugar Tongs. Josiah Penfield (1785–1828). *Ca.* 1820, American (Savannah). Silver. L. 6 1/2″ (16 1/4 cm.). Gift of Descombe Wells, 1961. Richardson-Owens-Thomas House Collection.

15b Sugar Tongs. Frederick Marquand (1799–1882). 1821, American (Savannah). Silver. L. 6 3/8″ (16.2 cm.). Gift of James A. Williams, 1968.

15c Sugar Tongs. Marquand and Co. (active in New York, 1833–1839). *Ca.* 1833–1839, American (New York). Silver. L. 6 1/8″ (15.5 cm.). Gift of James A. Williams, 1968.

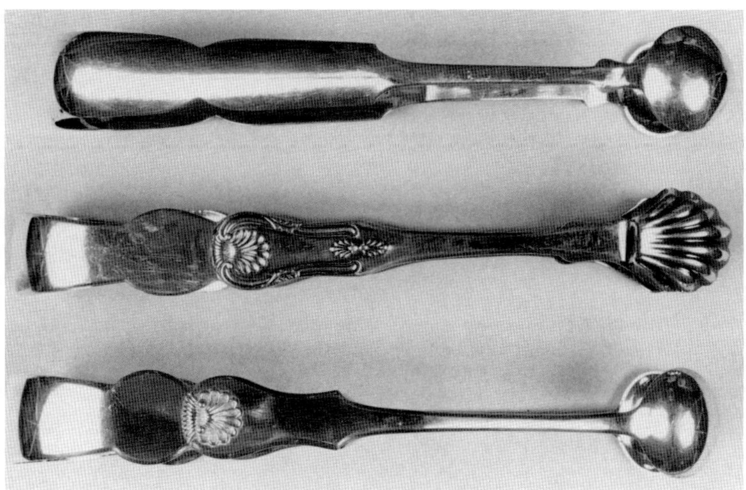

Top to bottom: 15a, 15b, 15c

Until the second quarter of the nineteenth century, silver utensils related to the service of tea and coffee were those most frequently found in the American home. A survey of estate inventories, 1800–1835, revealed sugar tongs as the most prevalent serving pieces other than spoons listed among the possessions of Savannahians. Successors of Isaac Marquand's firm produced the three pairs of sugar tongs found in the Telfair collection.

The pair made by Marquand and Co. exhibit fundamental classical features, a simple adaptation of the fiddleback spoon handle and unembellished round grippers. The decorative richness of the Empire style is more apparent in the shells and acorns used by Penfield and Marquand to enliven their designs that also incorporate variations on the fiddleback spoon handle.

Fish Knives

16a Fish Knife. Frederick Marquand (1799–1882). 1822, American (Savannah). Silver. L. 12 1/4″ (31.1 cm.). Gift of James A. Williams, 1968.

16b + Fish Knife. Heloise Boudo (active 1827–1837). *Ca.* 1827–1837, American (Charleston). Silver. L. 13 7/16″ (34.2 cm.). Gift of Mrs. Randolph Tobias, 1958. Richardson-Owens-Thomas House Collection.

16c Fish Knife. H. P. Horton (active in Savannah, 1850–1856). *Ca.* 1850, American (probably Savannah). Silver. L. 11 1/2″ (29.2 cm.). Gift of James A. Williams, 1968.

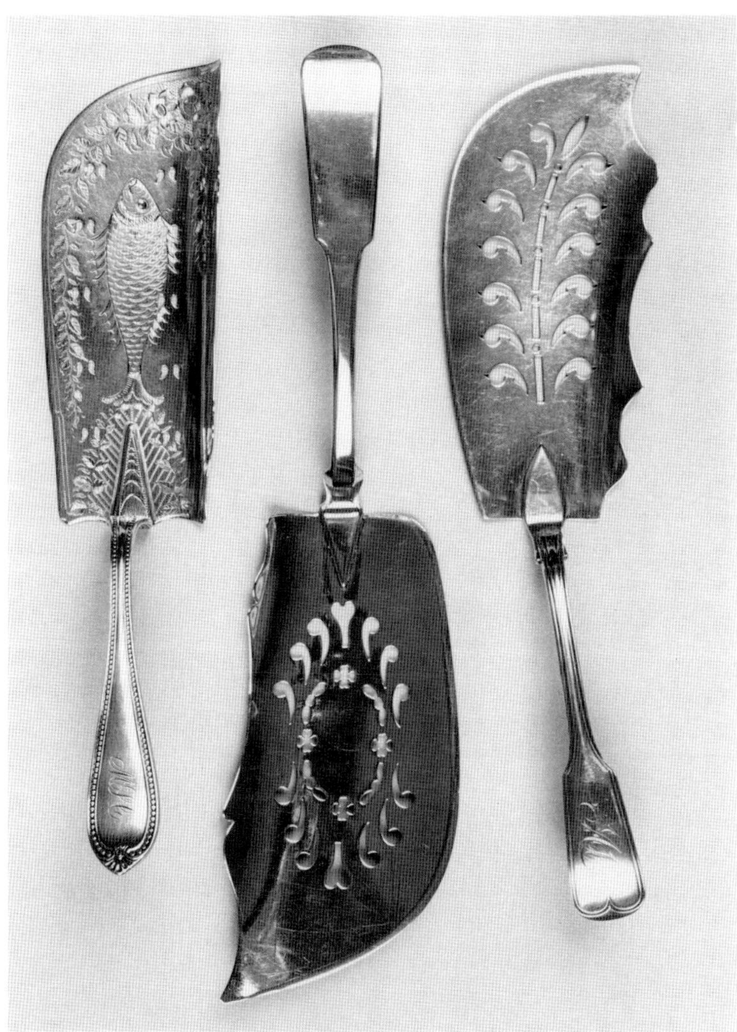

Left to right: 16c, 16b, 16a

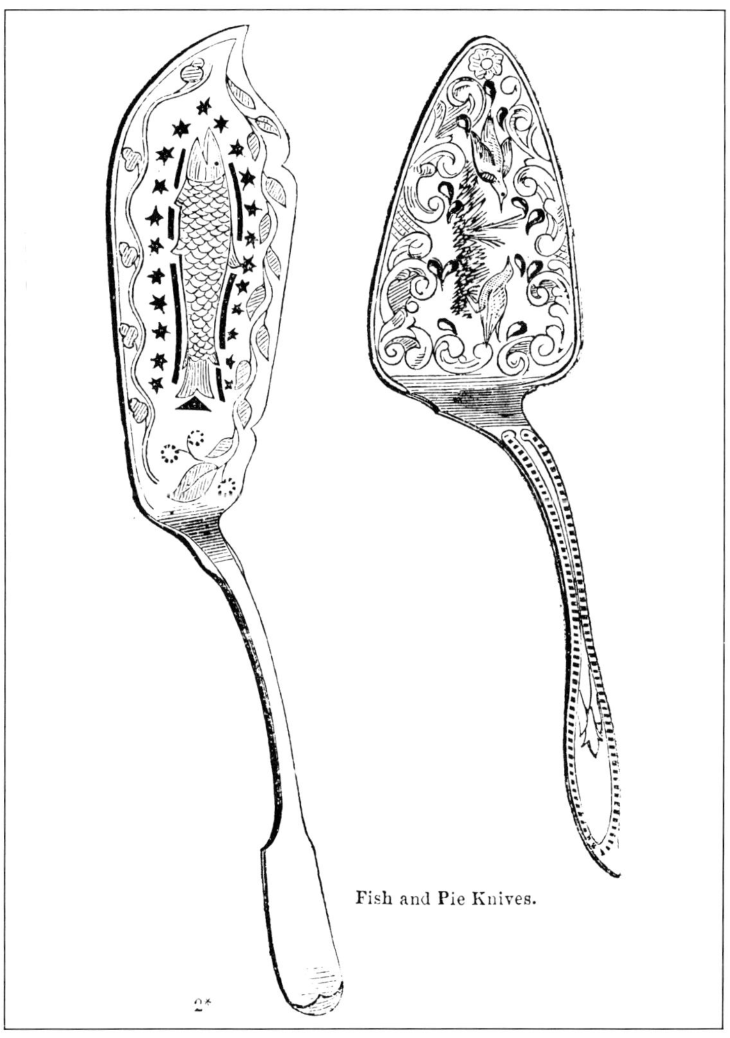

FIG. 25. Fish and pie knives, from R. E. Peterson and W. T. Peterson, *Catalogue of House Furnishing Goods, Stoves, Etc., Etc. . . .* (New York, 1857). (Courtesy of the Henry Francis du Pont Winterthur Museum Library: Collection of Printed Books and Periodicals.)

Guests at a nineteenth-century dinner entered the dining room to find the first course of soup, fish, and accompaniments set out on the table in a decorative and appetizing display. Showing valuable silver serving pieces, such as the soup ladle and fish knife, formed a significant part of the array that the host hoped would delight his guests. For this reason the fish knife was an important serving piece, so much so that silver ones are mentioned specifically in estate inventories.[37]

The three fish knives in the Telfair collection all bear the marks of Southern makers. Produced in 1822, the earliest was made by Frederick Marquand during his partnership with his cousin in the firm of Josiah Penfield and Co. This knife is part of a table service made for an unidentified patron.[38]

Heloise Boudo, who inherited the silversmithing and jewelry business of her husband, Louis, made a fish knife that is now in the Richardson-Owens-Thomas House Collection. Her Charleston firm was actively involved in both smithing and reselling the manufactures of other artisans, as was the common practice. Pieces manufactured by Boudo bore her mark alone, while pieces purchased for resale from other smiths were struck with the marks of Boudo and the supplier.

H. P. Horton was a relatively short-term figure on the scene in Savannah from 1850 until 1856. By 1850 the heyday of the independent silversmith had passed. Large companies were absorbing individual craftsmen into the burgeoning manufacturing system. In fact Horton's fish knife was not unique in design. Trade catalogs of mass-produced goods advertised almost identical fish knives (fig. 25) with a simple pierced pattern and engraved decoration depicting scrolling foliage and a fish.

37. Inventories of Philip Brosch (1825), Alexander Telfair (1833), John Williamson (1843), and Henry McAlpin (1851).

38. See cat. #17.

Table Services

17. Partial Table Service. Frederick Marquand (1799–1882). 1822, American (Savannah). Silver. Comprising 11 teaspoons: l. 6″ (15.1 cm.); 5 dessert spoons: l. 7 1/8″ (18.1 cm.); 9 tablespoons: l. 8 3/4″ (22.2 cm.); 4 luncheon forks: l. 7″ (17.8 cm.); and 11 dinner forks: l. 8 1/8″ (20.6 cm.); all monogrammed "AL." Gift of James A. Williams, 1968.

Silver table services as they are known today were a rarity in the early nineteenth century. Teaspoons and tablespoons were the most common items of flat silver, with ladles as the most numerous of the serving pieces. Horn, bone, and ivory rather than silver were standard materials for the handles of knives and forks.[39] The emergence of the dinner service made of matching forks, knives, spoons, and serving pieces seems to have paralleled the contemporaneous taste for decorating rooms *en suite*.

Frederick Marquand's legacy of high style silver suggests that he arrived in Savannah under the strong influence of the New York practice. In 1820, the year he turned twenty-one, Marquand came south to join the firm of his cousin Josiah Penfield. Marquand was probably fresh from completing his apprenticeship in New York, where his father stood at the hub of commerce. There, young Frederick undoubtedly had been exposed to the most fashionable American products and English imports. Further, he seems to have had a flair for style and salesmanship because he found a market in Savannah for wares not typically produced by Savannah smiths.

39. A traveler in upstate New York noted that "with the exception of the spoons, there is no silver on the table; the forks have two steel prongs, and their handles, like those of the knives, are of buck's horn" (Bernard Karl, Duke of Saxe-Weimar Eisenach, *Travels Through North America During the Years 1825–1826* [1828], p. 66).

17 (*front view, left to right*): Luncheon fork, dinner fork, tablespoon, dessert spoon, teaspoon

17 (*back view*)

Forks

18a Luncheon Forks (10). Moses Eastman (1794–1850). *Ca.* 1826–1850, American (Savannah). Silver. L. 6 5/8" (16.8 cm.). Gift of James A. Williams, 1968.

18b Luncheon Forks (12). Moses Eastman (1794–1850). *Ca.* 1835–1850, American (Savannah). Silver. L. 6 3/4" (17.2 cm.). Bequest of Gertrude West Hollowbush, 1988.

18c + Dinner Forks (6). H. P. Horton (active in Savannah 1850–1856). *Ca.* 1850–1856, American (Savannah). Silver. L. 7 13/16" (19.8 cm.). Gift of Descombe Wells, 1961. Richardson-Owens-Thomas House Collection.

18d Dinner Fork. Samuel Wilmot (active in Savannah 1850–1856). *Ca.* 1850–1856, American (Savannah). Silver. L. 8 1/8" (20.7 cm.). Gift of James A. Williams, 1968.

Like knives and full dinner services, silver forks were relative latecomers to the American silversmith's repertoire. Customarily stored in knife cases on the sideboard rather than with the silver, forks and knives had steel blades and tines, and bone, buck (that is, horn), or ivory handles. "Green handle knives and forks," like those of William Gibbons, were ivory stained with a green dye.[40]

Silver forks were seldom found among the belongings of residents of small cities like Savannah during the first quarter of the nineteenth century. Only one Savannahian in the survey whose inventory dated before 1825 owned silver forks.[41] Since a scant five rather than a dozen were listed, it is doubtful that these forks were part of a dinner set. Sets of silver forks, usually in multiples of twelve, are listed in five inventories dating between 1832 and 1843.[42] All of the silver forks in the Telfair collection also date after 1825.

Front view, left to right: 18b, 18a

Back view, left to right: 18b, 18a

Front view, left to right: 18c, 18d

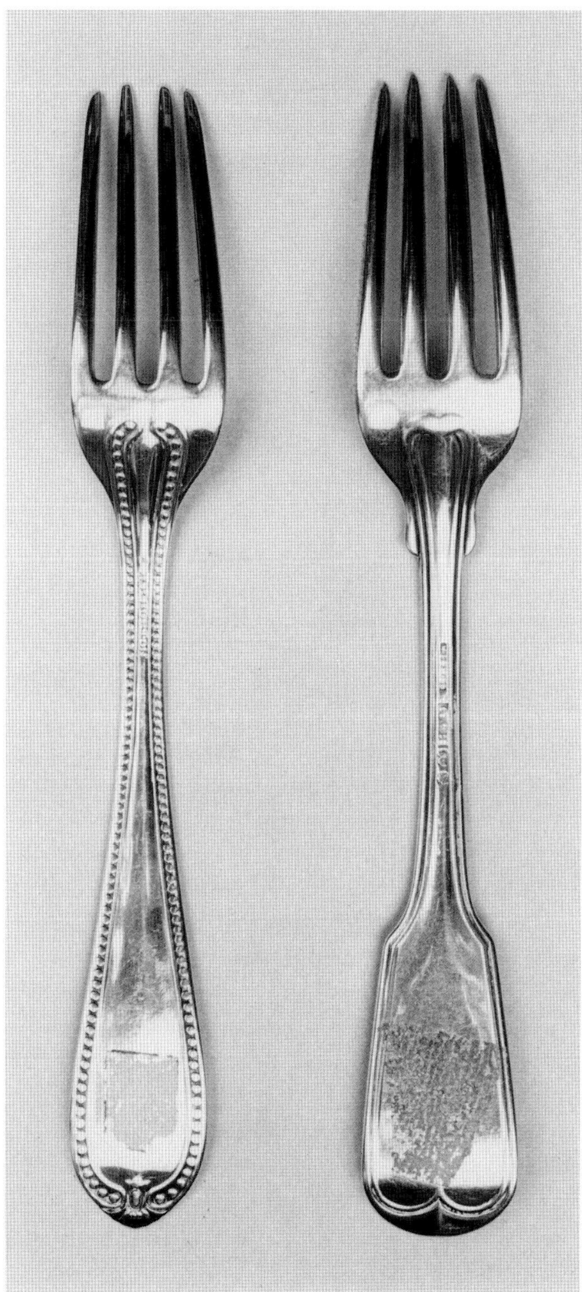

Back view, left to right: 18c, 18d

40. Inventory of William Gibbons (1803).
41. Inventory of John Courvoisie (1817).
42. Inventories of Joseph Habersham (1832), Priscilla Houstoun (1837), Richard Habersham (1842), John Williamson (1843), and Henry McAlpin (1851).

HOLLOWARE
Wine Paraphernalia

19a + Siphon. James Gilsland (active 1748–1763). *Ca.* 1759–1760, Scottish (Edinburgh). Silver. L. 15 1/2″ (39.3 cm.). Gift of Mrs. Samuel Varnedoe, 1962. Richardson-Owens-Thomas House Collection.

19b + Punch Strainer. Silver. Probably John Coburn (1725–1803). *Ca.* 1775, American (Boston). L. 11 3/16″ (28.4 cm.). Gift of Frances Noble Jones Luquer, 1960. Richardson-Owens-Thomas House Collection.

19c Funnel. Attributed to Thomas Fletcher and Sidney Gardiner (active in Philadelphia and Boston 1808–1827). *Ca.* 1810, American (Philadelphia). Silver. H. 6 5/8″ (16.8 cm.). Bequest of Mary Telfair, 1875.

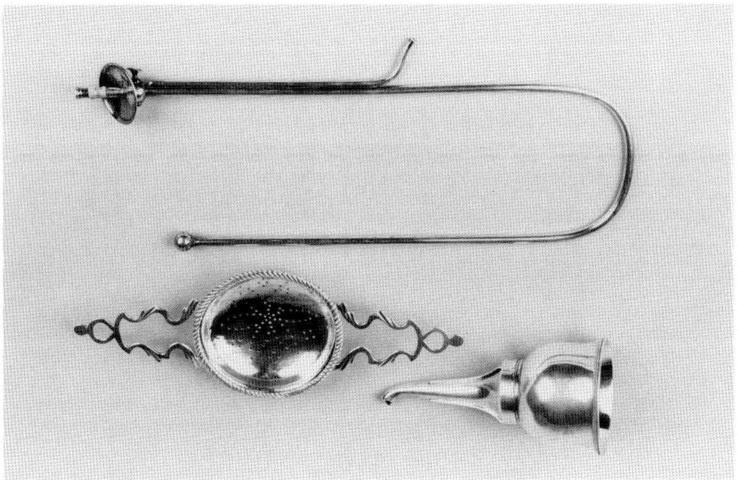

Top to bottom: 19a, 19b, 19c

Wine, particularly Madeira, has often been considered a significant lubricant of Southern hospitality. During the first half of the nineteenth century, many staples, including spirits, were purchased in large quantities. Buying wine by the pipe, barrel, or demijohn called for specialized equipment such as siphons and funnels for bottling and decanting at home.

Between 1800 and 1850 sizable stores of alcohol consistently appeared in Savannah inventories. Inevitably, conviviality was not the only effect of consuming spirits. For example, Jeremiah Evarts observed:

> I have resided now three days on a sea-island plantation, where I was treated with all the hospitality which the owner was master of. The house was large, the rooms airy, the furniture costly, the provisions of the table profusely abundant. . . . The master of the house was incapable of society from drinking brandy, and consequent stupidity and ignorance. He had been educated at Princeton college, and is probably somewhat under 40. Every evening he is so far overcome with strong drink, as to be silly, every morning, full of pain, languor, and destitute of appetite. The state of the slaves, as physical, intellectual, and moral beings, is abject beyond my powers of description; yet the state of the master is more to be pitied, as it exposes him to a more aggravated condemnation.[43]

Precisely as Jeremiah Evarts' commentary implies, there was almost always a connection between temperance and abolitionist movements. As a result, the impulse toward societal reform that swept the North made very little headway in the South.[44]

43. Diary of Jeremiah Evarts.

44. In 1831 44 percent of the nation's population lived in the South, but only 8.5 percent of the temperance pledges came from the region. Ian Tyrrell, "Drink and Temperance in the Antebellum South: An Overview and Interpretation," in *Journal of Southern History*, **48,** 4 (November 1982), pp. 485–510.

20

20* Cake Basket. Attributed to William Plummer (active 1755–1791). *Ca.* 1771–1772, English (London). Silver. L. 14 11/16" (37.2 cm.). Gift of Minnie H. Coulson, 1980.

An ornament for the tea or dining table, the cake basket often served as a focal point of the dessert course, the climax of a festive dinner party. Such costly silver items were by no means universally found in the households of Savannah's upper class. Out of twenty-six inventories meeting the criteria for elegant dining, only two listed silver cake baskets. Alexander Telfair owned one "cake basket, silver," while Henry McAlpin possessed four.[45] The advent of Sheffield plate brought cake baskets within the grasp of more American consumers. Even so, only a total of six plated cake baskets appeared in three of the sample inventories.[46] Yet cake baskets were for sale in Savannah. Among the dazzling variety of goods advertised by Josiah Penfield on January 17, 1817, were "late arrivals from England, France, and New York, [including] cake and bread baskets, shell and gadroon borders."[47]

Not historically associated with Savannah or the Telfair family, this handsome object belongs to Rococo England. The pierced body is particularly well suited to the decorative function of the container, which was meant to show off the baked goods within. Relatively few sterling cake baskets, neither imports nor the production of American smiths, found their way into the hands of Americans.

45. Inventories of Alexander Telfair (1833) and Henry McAlpin (1851).

46. Inventories of Delia Bryan (1827), Joseph Stiles (1839), and John Williamson (1843).

47. Penfield undoubtedly benefited from the far-reaching mercantile interests of his uncle and business colleague, Issac Marquand. No doubt Marquand, who was based in New York in 1816, supplied the goods enumerated in Penfield's advertisement as follows:

> *The subscriber has received* by late arrivals from England,
> France, and New-York, (Josiah Penfield)
> —2 elegant silver coffee and tea sets, 5 pieces each;
> silver cream jugs, Tumblers & pulp [pap] Boats,
> silver table, tea, soup and gravy Spoons
> silver sugar Tongs, butter knives & caddie spoons;
> silver coral and Bells, pencil cases, thimbles, Tooth Picks,
> 6 pair doubleplated four and six light Branches; silver
> Gadroons & elegant candlesticks and Brackets,
> silveredged & plain, a great variety;

cordial stands, 2 to 4 bottles, richly cut,
Gadroon and shell borders;
Cake and Bread Baskets, shell & gadroon borders;
Stands, Snuffers & Stands, fine Razors, pen Knives
Scissors & Lancets; plated & gilt sabres, small swords,
Dirks pistols, Epaulets & Laces, sword & plain Sticks, Whips
and Spurs, fire dogs, Shovels, Tongs, & Fenders, gilt &
plated ball Buttons & button rings, Indispensables,
pocketbooks & Purses, a handsome assortment of gentlemen's
Portable Shaving Cases, violin strings, hair and Pocket
Combs 600 yards India paper Hangings, richly gilt suitable
for drawing rooms, nearly as low as common paper

Josiah Penfield.

(*The Savannah Republican* [January 18, 1817], p. 4, col. 1.)

Tea and Coffee Services

21a Partial Tea and Coffee Service (3 pieces).[48] Harvey Lewis and Joseph Smith (active in Philadelphia 1805–1811). *Ca.* 1810,[49] American (Philadelphia). Silver. Coffee pot with additional filter: h. 14″ (35.5 cm.); teapot: h. 7 1/2″ (19 cm.); sugar bowl and cover: h. 7 7/8″ (20 cm.). Gifts of Hesse Pringle, Mitchell Troy, Sarah H. Pinney, and H. Rees Mitchell, respectively, 1986.

21b+Tea Service (4 pieces).[50] John Crawford (active in New York 1815–1836, Philadelphia 1837–1843). *Ca.* 1815–1820, American (New York). Silver. Teapot: h. 9 1/2″ (24.1 cm.); waste bowl: diam. 6″ (15.2 cm.); sugar bowl and cover: h. 8 3/4″ (22.2 cm.); cream pitcher: h. 7 5/8″ (19.3 cm.). Museum purchase, 1956. Richardson-Owens-Thomas House Collection.

21c Sugar Bowl and Cover. John McMullin (1765–1843). *Ca.* 1815–1825, American (Philadelphia). Silver. H. 8 3/4″ (22.3 cm.). Gift of Mrs. Barnwell Cubbedge, 1972.

21d Tea and Coffee Service (5 pieces). Thomas Whartenby (active in Philadelphia 1811–1850). *Ca.* 1825, American (Philadelphia). Silver. Coffee pot: h. 14″ (35.5 cm.); teapot: h. 11″ (28 cm.); teapot: h. 11 3/4″ (29.8 cm.); sugar bowl with cover: h. 11″ (28 cm.); cream pitcher: h. 7 1/8″ (18.1 cm.). Gift of Mr. Ernest Williams, 1986.

The neoclassicism of the Federal and Empire styles began to sweep the United States late in the eighteenth century and remained dominant until the 1840's. By the second decade of the nineteenth century, the Federal style was giving way to the new forms of the Empire taste. Four firms, one of New York and three of Philadelphia, are represented in the Telfair collection by tea and coffee services or partial services. In each example the chaste verticality of abstracted vases characteristic of the Federal style has given way to the bulbous, more horizontal bodies and pedestal bases of the Empire. With the advent of the Empire, bright-cut and geometric details such as gadrooning and beading decreased in popularity while more exuberant naturalistic foliate motifs gained favor.

The objects in the Telfair collection made by McMullin and by Lewis and Smith retain a few features of the passing Federal taste. There are disproportionately light bands of gadrooning and engraved decoration. The handles of several pieces look spindly on the rounded, heavy bodies. The manufactures of Whartenby and Crawford, on the other hand, reveal the Empire style in full flower. Here the bulbous bodies are set off by sculpted and cast decorations, such as scrolled handles, bud and foliate finials, and robust bands of flora.

The popularity of tea and coffee in the nineteenth century is evidenced by the elaborate and expensive wares produced for its service as well as by a lively literature outlining genteel methods of brewing and serving the beverages. At the beginning of the century there were a number of innovations in the technology of steeping coffee. Count Rumford invented a pot that worked by infusion.[51] One Mr. Biggin gave his name to a forerunner of the percolator.[52]

The coffee pot of the Lewis and Smith set is fitted with several accessories that are seldom seen in silver services. These rare survivals are the mechanisms for brewing coffee according to the designs of Rumford and Biggin. In addition to the body and top, the coffee pot is equipped with two cylindrical vessels with open tops and perforated bottoms. The smaller cylinder fits snugly into the slightly larger one, which in turn rests in the top opening of the pot. According to Count Rumford's method, coffee was placed in the larger cylinder. The smaller cylinder was then pressed into the larger cylinder to compact the coffee. Hot water was poured into the smaller vessel and allowed to seep through the coffee into the main body of the pot below.

Because the form of the coffee pot is so unusual, Lewis and Smith probably made it according to the special instructions of their clients Elizabeth and Thomas Rice of White Bluff near Savannah. If so, they were not the only Savannahians to take special interest in making coffee by the latest methods. William Gibbons specifically notes "one coffee pot or biggen" and "my silver coffee biggin" in a household inventory and in his will, respectively.[53]

It was customary for Southerners to place orders for silver with Northern craftsmen when they made their annual migrations to escape the deadly fevers of the Southern summer. Just as the Rices and the Richardsons purchased silver from Lewis and Smith and from John Crawford, the Savannahian William Gibbons patronized a number of craftsmen in the summer of 1802. Happily, a detailed record of his transactions has survived.[54] He paid the silversmith Thomas Warren $87 for "1 silver sugar dish and

21a

21b

21c

21d

cream pot." Later he made additional purchases of hollowware and flat silver. In each case he entered specific sums for materials, fabrication, and engraving. Like many silversmiths, Warren must have purchased metalwares from other makers for resale, since Gibbons also purchased ivory forks, table and dessert knives, and carvers as well as brass andirons, tongs, and a shovel from Warren.

48. According to family tradition, the set originally included a creamer that was lost in a fire. See Sally Pinney letter to Ann Miller, August 9, 1985 (Telfair Academy Accession File 1986.2–4).

49. Family history holds that the tea service was made for Elizabeth Dews and Thomas Rice on the occasion of their marriage at Christ Church, Philadelphia, in 1792. Stylistic evidence and the records of the partnership of Lewis and Smith suggest a later date. Further, a tea service that is comprised of more pieces, but is identical in form, was made by James Howell for the wealthy Philadelphian Henry Pratt in 1811.

50. Tradition has it that this tea service was a gift to Frances Lewis Bolton, a Savannahian, on the occasion of her marriage to Richard Richardson on December 10, 1811. The letter "R" is engraved on each piece, and "F. L. B. Richardson" is scratched on the interior of the teapot. Since Crawford is not recorded as being in business before 1815, the service was probably not a wedding gift. It is possible that the tea service was commissioned for the Richardsons' home (now the Richardson-Owens-Thomas House), which was completed in 1819.

51. Thomas Webster, *An Encyclopedia of Domestic Economy* (1845), p. 712.

52. Edward Wenham, *Domestic Silver of Great Britain and Ireland* (1931), p. 102.

53. Account book of William Gibbons (1802–1804) and will of William Gibbons (1803). Plated and Britannia biggins appear in the inventory of Joseph Clay (1805) and the inventory of Henry McAlpin (1851), respectively.

54. Account book of William Gibbons (1802–1804).

22 Pap Boat. William Thomson (active in New York 1810–1833, 1841–1845). *Ca.* 1815, American (New York). Silver. L. 5 3/4" (14.5 cm.). Gift of Mr. William K. Wallbridge, 1959.

William Thomson spent his working life in New York. As the provenance of the Telfair pap boat attests, Southerners patronized Thomson's New York shop. A christening cup that bears his mark and that of a Natchez maker suggests that he also sent his wares to Southern craftsmen for resale.[55]

Even though pap boats are not ordinarily found in American silver, Thomson is known to have made two. One is in the collection of the Metropolitan Museum of Art,[56] and the other is owned by the Telfair. Both are shaped with the gentle, clean lines characteristic of Thomson's approach to neoclassicism, which is expressed in the conventions of the Federal rather than the Empire style. This simple aesthetic is particularly well suited to the humble function of the pap boat. These vessels were used for feeding soft foods to infants and invalids.

The Telfair pap boat is engraved with the name of George Haig. It may have belonged to the invalid husband of Sarah Telfair Haig, but it was more probably a baby gift to their son, also named George Haig. The father died in 1815, before the child was born; and the little boy did not survive until his second birthday. Not an isolated tragedy, the fate of father and son was an all too frequent course of events in the nineteenth century.

22

55. Winterthur Museum, Decorative Arts Photo Archive, file on William Thomson.

56. MBD [Marshall B. Davidson], "American Silver of the Early Nineteenth Century," in *Bulletin of the Metropolitan Museum of Art, 34*, 1 (January 1939), p. 26.

23* Tray. *Ca.* 1815, English (Sheffield). Silver plate. L. 30" (76.2 cm.). Gift of friend's of the late Mrs. Louise Lehardy, 1960.

Because large items made of sterling were beyond the means of most consumers, makers of more reasonably priced Sheffield plate found a natural market for larger goods—trays, urns, epergnes, candelabra, and so forth—such as those shown on the trade card of Ashforth, Cutts, and Anderton (fig. 26). Striving to creatively exploit this demand, early nineteenth-century makers of Sheffield excelled in the design and manufacture of trays. Makers offered a great array of borders, feet, and handles to offset chased or plain grounds according to the customer's desire.

23

Fig. 26. Trade card of Ashforth, Cutts, and Anderton, from *A New, General, and Commercial Directory of Sheffield and Its Vicinity* (Manchester, England, 1825). (Courtesy of the Henry Francis du Pont Winterthur Museum Library: Collection of Printed Books and Periodicals.)

24

24* Soup Tureen and Cover. Attributed to Philip Rundell (1743–1827). 1819, English (London). Silver. L. 18 3/4″ (47.6 cm.). Gift of the Minis Estate, 1938.

Among the many delectables that could make up the first course of fish and soup, turtle was a great favorite with Savannahians. Whereas Savannah was well known for supplying the country with terrapins in the later nineteenth and twentieth centuries, Savannahians feasted on the Bahamian green turtle in earlier days. In June 1801 Robert Mackay wrote to his wife that he had received as a gift "the finest turtle I ever saw in Georgia, it weighed 80 pounds and was literally fat as butter."[57] A few lines down, Mackay noted his dinner companions' appreciation of the fine turtle: "Gibbons was delighted and swallowed green fat in platefuls—Woodruff looked charmed and confessed approbation by inarticulating silence, Nichols thought he had the calipash to serve out, took great care to serve himself plentifully and as to Caig, as Burns says in his poem of the Haggis, 'He was like to rive.'"[58]

Later, writing to his wife in 1845, Dr. Richard Arnold remarked on another turtle prepared to perfection, where never was "more ample justice done to the succulent qualities of that first and best of the forbidden things of Moses. The stew was composed entirely of the green fat of the Turtle and the forced-meat balls were made out of the muscular part. Nothing foreign marred the taste. Spice enough to season without stimulation, and madeira and claret enough to mingle with its own juices and form a rich gravy were all the seasoning."[59] Those not fortunate enough to procure a turtle to cook at home could respond to professional cooks like Sylvia Waitfield, who announced "A fine fat Bahama green Turtle will be dressed on Tuesday next, at 11 o:clock. . . . Families supplied by sending."[60]

This tureen is a repository equal to the most sumptuous of turtle dishes, yet it is highly unlikely that the original owner was a Savannahian. Such an article certainly was created for the English market. It is a fine expression of Regency England, articulated with taste and assurance. The horizontality of the ellipsoidal body is agreeably balanced by the loop handles and scroll feet. Classical details, such as the lobes and the molded lion's heads and foliage, complete the piece with sophistication and grace.

57. Walter Charlton Hartridge, Jr., ed., *The Letters of Robert Mackay to His Wife, Written From Ports in America and England, 1795–1816* (1949), pp. 30–31.
58. *Ibid.*, p. 31. Calipash is a greenish, jellylike, edible substance under the upper shell of a turtle.
59. Richard H. Shryock, ed., *Letters to Richard D. Arnold, M. D., 1808–1876, . . .* (1929), p. 26.
60. *The Republican and Savannah Evening Ledger* (May 20, 1815), p. 4.

25

25* Coffee Urn. *Ca.* 1820, English (Sheffield). Silver plate. H. 16 5/8" (42.2 cm.). Gift of James A. Williams, 1967.

Tea and coffee urns were popular items made in Sheffield plate for domestic and foreign consumption. Manufacturers of plate offered a variety of designs for urns similar to the one in the Telfair collection (fig. 27). In 1802 a Savannah newspaper carried an advertisement announcing: "On Consignment—Just received by the Cleopatra from London . . . 12 neat Tea and Coffee Urns, Elegantly finished. FOR SALE by DICKSON & JOHNSTON."[61] In 1803 the Savannahian William Gibbons bequeathed to his brother Barack Gibbons "one tea boiler and coffee urn."[62] Both functional and ceremonial, the urn was used at family meals, particularly breakfast. If the family preferred tea, the urn was filled with water that was in turn emptied into the teapot. If coffee was the beverage of choice, the cups were filled from the urn.

Keeping the contents of the urn warm was an important consideration, and designers devised several methods for accomplishing this end. The Telfair urn was equipped with a metal sleeve and an ingot not unlike a sash weight. Miss Leslie advised: "In preparing the urn, see that the heater is put into the fire in time to become red-hot."[63] The English instructor of servants, Thomas Cosnett, went further:

> You must always have the urn nearly full of water, or coffee, if the heater be very hot, or else it will burn the urn and do it harm: put the heater into it gently, or you will in time knock out the bottom of the urn: when the end of the hook you put it in with is worn off, have it fresh done, for many urns get spoiled through using tongs instead of a proper hook, by which the heater is suffered to fall into the urn with such force as often spoils it.[64]

Cosnett's word to wise servants shows that the red-hot ingot was not an ideal technology for keeping an urn warm. On top of all the pitfalls that Cosnett outlined, the ingot was not apt to keep the contents warm for very long. When someone devised small

FIG. 27. Design for a coffee urn, from Christ Wilson, *Book of Silver Patterns* (London, *ca.* 1820). (Courtesy of the Henry Francis du Pont Winterthur Museum Library: Collection of Printed Books and Periodicals.)

spirit lamps to place underneath the urn, the innovation was welcomed by both master and servant and gained widespread popularity.

61. *The Columbian Museum and Savannah Advertiser* (June 22, 1802), p. 3.
62. Will of William Gibbons (1803). Other coffee urns listed in the inventories surveyed are as follows: "one plated coffee urn," Philip Brosch (1825); one large and one small silver urn with a combined value calculated by weight to be $227.61, Joseph Stiles (1839); and one large coffee urn worth $157, John Williamson (1843).
63. Eliza Leslie, *The House Book: . . .* (1841), p. 275.
64. Thomas Cosnett, *The Footman's Directory and Butler's Remembrancer* (1823), p. 70.

26 Water Pitcher. Frederick Marquand (1799–1882). 1824, American (Savannah). Silver. H. 13 1/4" (33.6 cm.). Gift of James A. Williams, 1968.

Frederick Marquand seems to have had a knack for luring Savannah's most sophisticated and fashionable consumers. His oeuvre is accented with pieces in unusual and expensive forms for which other Savannah silversmiths seldom won commissions.[65] For example, a check of selected inventories taken in Savannah between 1800 and 1855 yielded only three silver water pitchers.[66]

The Telfair water pitcher eloquently states Marquand's grasp of the Empire style. The widely flaring spout and richly rounded body are balanced by the vigorously scrolling handle embellished by cast foliage. Cast ornamentation, a major decorative element of the Empire period, is used throughout the piece. Marquand achieved a sculptural, almost monumental, effect in the water pitcher, which made it an impressive ornament for the table of its owner.

26

65. See cat. 16, 17, and 27 for discussions of a fish knife, table service, and toast rack by Frederick Marquand.
66. Inventories of Francis Doyle (1817), Joseph Stiles (1839), and John Williamson (1843).

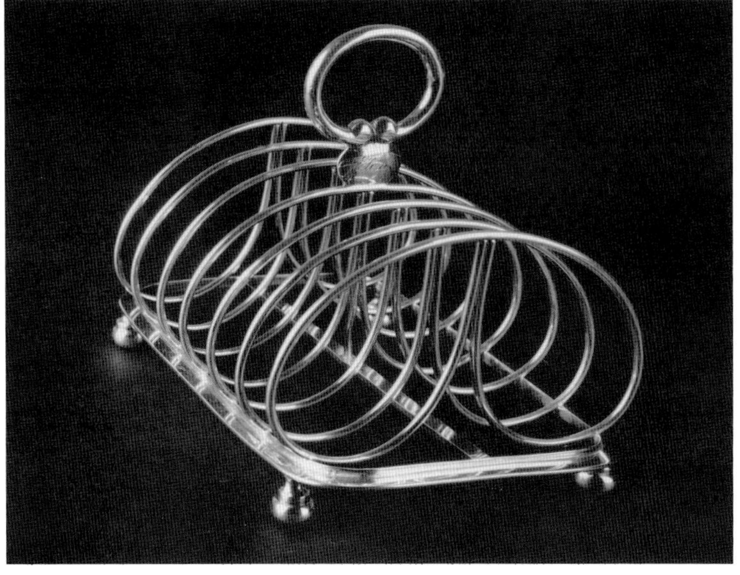

27

27 Toast Rack. Frederick Marquand (1799–1882). 1825, American (Savannah). Silver. H. 5 1/8″ (13 cm.); l. 6 11/16″ (17 cm.); w. 4 3/8″ (11.1 cm.). Museum purchase, 1980.

Toast racks became popular in England around 1770, but did not catch on in the United States until the beginning of the nineteenth century. Even then they were not found in many households. Only one toast rack appeared in a sampling of estate inventories taken in Savannah between 1800 and 1855.[67] It is reasonable to guess that Marquand made this toast rack for one of Savannah's most style-conscious citizens.

Marquand's production of modish objects hints at some pretension on the part of the smith or his clients. This idea is reinforced by his manner of marking objects. The marks of most American smiths included the maker's initials or surname and possibly the name of a city. A few silversmiths created adaptations of English hallmarks, substituting an eagle for the leopard, a bust of Washington for the monarch, a star from the flag for the lion. However, early nineteenth-century New York silversmiths, including Marquand, unabashedly appropriated English pseudo-hallmarks like those found on this toast rack, which is touched with Marquand's initials, a bust, a date letter, and a lion.[68]

67. Inventory of Barack Gibbons (1814). This toast rack valued at $.25 was most certainly not made of silver.

68. Martha Gandy Fales, *Early American Silver* (1970), p. 247.

28 Waiter. Samuel Kirk (1792–1872). 1828, American (Baltimore). Silver. Diam. 9″ (22.8 cm.). Bequest of Mary Telfair, 1875.

Samuel Kirk was trained under the guidance of James Howell in Philadelphia. Upon completion of his apprenticeship in 1815, Kirk moved to Baltimore, where he worked in partnership with John Smith until 1821. In the course of his long career, which stretched from 1815 until 1872, Kirk became the most important Maryland silversmith of the day. His wares, which were very sought after, accounted for great percentages of silver recorded at the Baltimore assay office annually.[69]

In 1828, the year that the Telfair waiter was made, Kirk is credited with ninety-three percent of the silver registered at the assay office. In the same year he made four similar waiters, which are now in museum collections.[70] In each instance Kirk decorated the field with a "pricked" star pattern that encloses a meandering grapevine. He employed various classical motifs for the borders and raised each of the salvers on three feet.

Kirk's capacity for innovative design expanded the technical vocabulary of his American contemporaries. During the 1830's he

28

29

made his most far-reaching advance by initiating a revival of the ancient technique of repoussé. By mid-century this technique, coupled with the inevitable stylistic outgrowths, was at the forefront of a new fashion in American silver.

69. The Baltimore Museum of Art, *Eighteenth and Nineteenth Century Maryland Silver in the Collection of the Baltimore Museum of Art* (1975), p. 136.

70. Similar salvers are found in the collections of the Baltimore Museum of Art, the Metropolitan Museum of Art, and the Peale Museum.

29* Cruet Stand with Castors. John Settle and Henry Wilkinson[71] (active *ca.* 1828–1830). 1830, English (Sheffield). Silver, glass. Stand: h. 10 1/8″ (25.7 cm.). Bequest of Miss Margaret Thomas, 1951. Richardson-Owens-Thomas House Collection.

While the name of John Settle appeared as a silversmith in Sheffield city directories from 1815 until 1830, his partnership with Henry Wilkinson lasted only from 1828 until Settle retired around 1830. After his partner's retirement, Wilkinson carried on in business under his own name. The firms with which Settle was associated were known for manufactures in both silver and Sheffield plate in a fairly wide variety of forms. In Savannah inventories cruet frames were almost equally divided between sterling and its more affordable substitute, plate.[72]

Because cruet stands with castors went onto the table with each meal, servants' manuals specifically detailed their care. These instructions give an account of which condiments went to the table and how the nineteenth-century servant met concerns for freshness and cleanliness:

> The Cruet-Stand must be looked to every day, to see that there is a sufficiency of mustard, oil, vinegar, or any other kind of sauces which there are glasses for. Let the mustard, vinegar, or any thing else which will spoil through keeping, be used in the kitchen before it is kept too long, and fresh put into the cruet stand: this will prevent any waste, and keep your cruet-stand in proper order. A paper cover for the cruet-stand may be easily made, which will keep it from the dust, or being tarnished by the damp air.[73]

71. Seymour Wyler and other American sources list Henry Wilkinson as Henry Williamson. Bradbury and Sheffield city directories, however, record the name as Wilkinson.

72. These inventories listed silver castors: Edward Telfair (1808), Philip Brosch (1825), Joseph Stiles (1839), and Henry McAlpin (1851). Plated castors appeared in these inventories: William Gibbons (1804), Barack Gibbons (1814), John Gibbons (1816), Francis Doyle (1817), George Haig (1817), and Priscilla Houstoun (1837).

73. Other condiments found in the cruet frame might be cayenne and Jamaica pepper, powdered loaf sugar, soy and fish sauces, chutney, and walnut or mushroom catsup. Tomato catsup, however, was a relative late comer to the table. See Thomas Cosnett, *The Footman's Directory, . . .* (1823), pp. 68–69.

III. Ceramics and Glass

30* Partial Dinner Service (51 pieces). Josiah Wedgwood's factory. *Ca.* 1785–1800, English (Etruria, Staffordshire). Hand-painted and gilt glazed earthenware. Pieces shown: soup plate: diam. 9 3/4″ (24.8 cm.); dinner plate: diam. 9 3/4″ (24.8 cm.); vegetable dish (no cover): l. 9 5/8″ (24.2 cm.); vegetable dish and cover: h. 4 3/4″ (12.1 cm.), l. 9 3/8″ (23.8 cm.); small tureen with cover: h. 5″ (12.7 cm.); tureen stand: diam. 6 11/16″ (17 cm.); platter with well: l. 18 3/8″ (46.7 cm.). Gift of Anderson C. Bouchelle, 1984.

Already a popular ceramic with the English consumer, Josiah Wedgwood's cream-colored earthenware received a promotional boost and the nickname "Queen's Ware" when Queen Charlotte ordered a set in 1762. Along with a flood of other English products, Queen's Ware entered the American market in the 1780's as the end of the Revolution allowed the renewal of trade.

During the post-revolutionary period, Americans discarded their pewter tableware in favor of new ceramic imports.[74] In this environment Josiah Wedgwood's Queen's Ware enjoyed an enormous share of the market. The basic cream-colored vessels, from which the wares drew their original name, were available in a wide range of choices for edge ornaments. Americans seemed to favor green, blue, and plain-edged pieces.[75] However, by the time of Wedgwood's death in 1795, the passion for Queen's Ware had passed its peak and his factory had entered a decline, only to reemerge after experimenting with the introduction of bone china in 1812.

Although it was somewhat old-fashioned by the beginning of the nineteenth century, Queen's Ware figured specifically in Savannah documents dating from between 1802 and 1842. William

30

Gibbons' household memorandum was the most detailed notation with references to a number of "green-edged" place and serving dishes. In 1808 and 1819 "One Lot of Queen's Ware" and "5 Queen's Ware dishes" were passed over summarily in the estate inventories of Edward Telfair and Noble Wimberly Jones, respectively. More than twenty years later Queen's Ware cropped up again, this time in the inventory of Richard Habersham, whose heirs would inherit not just a few odd pieces but a Queen's Ware "dinner set" appraised at $15, and a "China print set" and a "Dinner set" worth $30 each.[76]

74. Pewter is frequently found in Savannah inventories well into the nineteenth century. It held, however, a lowly position in the scheme of things—designated in lots with kitchenwares and such, obviously saved for humble uses long after its status in the household had diminished.

75. Helen Sprackling, *Customs of the Table Top: . . .* (1958), p. 6.

76. Inventory of Richard Habersham (1842).

31* Tea Service. Hollins, Warburton and Co. *Ca.* 1795–1810, English (New Hall, near Shelton, Staffordshire). Hand-painted and gilt porcelain, pattern #446. Pieces shown: Teapot: h. 6 1/16" (15.3 cm.); teapot stand: l. 6 11/16" (17 cm.); sugar bowl with cover: h. 4 3/4" (12 cm.); cream pitcher: h. 3 1/4" (8.2 cm.); waste bowl: diam. 5 15/16" (15 cm.); teacup (8): h. 2 1/4" (5.7 cm.); saucer (8): diam. 5 3/8" (13.7 cm.); saucer dish: diam. 8 3/8" (21.3 cm.). Gift of Robert E. Jones, 1983.

Because it was the staple refreshment at the heart of family life and hospitality in Western culture, tea persisted as the main export from China throughout the nineteenth century. Many Western industrialists prospered by catering to the taste for tea. Not the least of them were ceramics manufacturers who recognized that anyone who could afford a little something special for the household acquired a fancy tea set. People with means often owned a silver tea service as well as at least one or two ceramic ones.

The proprietors of the porcelain factory at New Hall found a niche in the ceramics market by producing tea (and other small) services for the well-fixed consumer. They sought the customer who might not have been able to afford silver or the finest porcelain, but who wanted something more refined than earthenware and more colorful than blue and white, the most typical forms of dinnerware.[77] This tea set exemplifies how New Hall met these needs. Basing the shapes of the serving pieces on silver forms imparted elegance, applying gilt suggested richness of decoration, and limiting the size of the set to eight cups insured a reasonable price.

A number of Savannahians fit exactly into the market to which the New Hall wares appealed, because gilt tea services are specified in estate documents.[78] The household account book of William

31

Gibbons reveals that he paid M. Shearrer $57 for a "set gilt Tea China" on March 11, 1802, even though he simultaneously owned two other china tea sets as well as silver tea wares. Many owners of gilt tea sets, however, owned little or no silver hollowware. For them the gilt tea set was undoubtedly the showpiece of the household.

77. David Holgate, *New Hall and Its Imitators* (1971), p. 16.
78. Household account book of William Gibbons (1802); and inventories of Edward Telfair (1808), Barack Gibbons (1814), Philip Brosch (1825), and Sarah Telfair (1828).

32+ Partial Dinner Service (128 pieces). *Ca.* 1820–1880, Chinese (Canton). Glazed earthenware. Pieces shown: creamer: h. 4 1/8″ (10.4 cm.), l. 7″ (17.8 cm.); tureen: l. 12 3/4″ (32.4 cm.); creamer: h. 4 3/8″ (11.1 cm.), l. 7 1/16″ (17.9 cm.); dinner plate: diam. 10 3/16″ (25.9 cm.); soup plate: diam. 8 3/4″ (22.2 cm.); cup: h. 3 7/8″ (9.1 cm.); saucer: diam. 5 3/4″ (14.6 cm.); fruit basket and stand: l. 8 5/8″ (21.9 cm.); sauce boat: l. 7 5/8″ (19.8 cm.); vegetable dish with cover: l. 10 3/4″ (27.3 cm.); platter: l. 14 9/16″ (37 cm.); vegetable dish with cover: l. 9 1/4″ (23.5 cm.); salad bowl: diam. 9 7/8″ (25 cm.); butter dish with cover: h. 7 3/16″ (18.3 cm.). Gift of Dr. Albert Galin, 1970. Richardson-Owens-Thomas House Collection.

The first cargo bound directly from China to an American port entered New York harbor in 1785. From that date the vogue for Canton ware grew until it reached its peak between 1820 and 1840 and completely ebbed by 1880. Much of the history of China trade ceramics has emphasized large, custom-ordered services that remained intact. Much more characteristic of everyday life was the buyer who may have purchased a modest service through a local retailer once in a lifetime and then continued to add specialty items and replacements over the years. Thus, one finds citations like those in the documents relating to William Gibbons' personalty. Gibbons made a bequest of "one broken set [blue] and white india china."[79] His household accounts refer to a payment to Marquand "for 1/2 doz blue and white breakfast cups."

Apparently the loss and breakage that necessitated the replacement of items was universal. The authors of domestic management manuals counseled young brides on how to minimize the risk by proposing rather complex devices for holding servants accountable for attrition. "A lady" advises:

32

> The breakage of glass, china, &c. of all sorts, forms an article of expense in every family, of which no calculation can be made: some servants are unlucky, some careless, and all liable to accidents. Where there is a number also, the evil sometimes becomes serious, and it is not confined merely to the expense of replacing what may be broken, but will probably be felt at the most inconvenient time. Just as you are ready to receive a party to dinner, you may be informed by the Cook, that she has not dishes enough; or the Footman may say, that there are not sufficient glasses and tumblers.[80]

The "lady's" remedy of this situation is a complicated system of inventories to be matched against timely confessions of breakage by the servants. Even these measures, the "lady" foresaw, would not be foolproof; but she hoped they might prove effective enough to forestall dire emergencies such as the one described above. And so it was that services evolved by attrition and replacement over the years.

32

Canton wares were available in both tea and table services, with the former usually numbering about fifty pieces and the latter ranging from one hundred and seventy to over two hundred pieces. Most estate documents pass over chinaware with the general designations a "lot" of this or a "sett" of that. Specific pieces are rarely cited.[81] As one might imagine, meals of several courses with many entrées required a substantial variety of place plates and serving pieces of every description.

This partial service gives a fair idea of the variety of sizes and shapes. Of course there are soup plates and a soup tureen for the first course. In addition there are place plates of various sizes, numerous octagonal and oval platters, and covered vegetable dishes. A three-piece butter dish combines an octagonal saucer with a circular, domed top. A circular, pierced plate fits into the bottom of the saucer to support the butter above cooling ice to keep it sweet. And there is an array of small pitchers and sauceboats for the essential sauces and gravies. A square salad bowl in William Gibbons' set has a parallel in this service.[82]

Coming after the puddings and pies, fresh fruits were the major component of the dessert course, the climax of any dinner party. Reticulated fruit baskets and stands made for a splendid presentation of the delicacies proffered by the host. Only two of the inventories included in our study explicitly cited fruit baskets.[83]

79. The name "India china"—that is, what is known as Canton ware today—derived from the monopoly that the British East India Company held over trade between China and Great Britain and her American colonies prior to the Revolution. "1 India china dinner set 225 pieces $25" appears in the inventory of Joseph Habersham (1832).

80. A Lady, *The Home Book; . . .* (1829), p. 34.

81. Individual pieces of china are named in the household memorandum of William Gibbons (1803); and in the inventories of Priscilla Houstoun (1837) and Henry McAlpin (1851).

82. Household memorandum of William Gibbons (1803).

83. Inventories of Philip Brosch (1825) and Henry McAlpin (1851).

Transfer Printed Wares

33a Partial Dinner Service. J. and W. Ridgway factory. Gravy tureen and stand. *Ca.* 1825, English (Staffordshire). Transfer printed earthenware. Tureen with cover: l. 8 1/4" (21 cm.); stand: l. 8 3/8" (21.3 cm.). Museum purchase, 1991.

33b* Partial Dinner Service. John Davenport's factory. *Ca.* 1825–1835, English (Longport, Staffordshire). Transfer printed earthenware. Tureen with cover: l. 13" (33.0 cm.); platter: l. 18 3/8" (46.7 cm.).

Practicality, and therefore marketability, distinguished English tablewares of the nineteenth century. Perhaps the greatest innovation of the industry was the development of transfer printing. Based on the precise duplication of a pattern by a semimechanical process, transfer printing assured quality of decoration at a price that could not be matched by hurried pieceworkers who mass-produced hand-painted wares.

English factories made ceramics in a wide variety of useful and ornamental shapes as well as an infinite number of surface designs. An advertisement of a Savannah enterprise, known as the "Staffordshire Ware-House," exemplifies the incredible number of English wares that were available in the United States during the 1820's. The ad, taken out by John Thomas on Tuesday morning, January 1, 1822, was not a mere snippet, but took up an entire column of small print in *The Savannah Museum*. Humble wares, suitable for the kitchen and lavatory, led the list with the finer items following. Painted mocha and black ware, edge ware, and luster delftware were all noted. The greatest part of the column, however, was given over to "Blue Printed Ware." For instance there were six hogsheads of cups, tea, dessert, breakfast, cake, and dinner plates; soups and flats of ten patterns; six hogsheads of "DOUBLE DINING SETS latest patterns, two hundred pieces to each set"; as well as similar double dining sets of "BRITISH VIEWS, patterns nearly all different and the engravings executed in a very superior style." Even this isolated advertisement in a regional newspaper shows how pervasive English blue transfer printed wares became in the American market.

The pattern of the Davenport service obviously draws on the decorative conventions of Canton ware—the pagoda, the river, and the willow trees. Clearly the designer has appealed as well to the exuberant taste of the 1830's by replacing the abstract Canton border with lush fruits, flowers, and foliage. Nearly all of the early blue-and-white transfer printed patterns derived from designs on Chinese porcelains. Nevertheless designers were soon

33a

33b

borrowing themes from topography, history, literature, and biology as well as chinoiserie.

In order to compete better for markets in the United States, English potters manufactured wares depicting American scenes in addition to the British views listed in the Savannah advertisement. For their "Beauties of America" series, John and William Ridgway selected engravings of buildings rather than picturesque landscape. Although most of the twenty or so buildings comprising the series were located in Boston, Philadelphia, and New York, the "Beauties of America" included a few buildings in Southern cities, such as the Exchange in Charleston and the Branch Bank of the United States in Savannah pictured on the gravy tureen.

The decoration of the tureen recalls two characters who appeared elsewhere in this text—Joshua Shaw and William Jay. The enterprising Shaw traveled in the South during 1819–1820 in order to gather materials and subscriptions for two or three publications: *United States Directory, Picturesque Views of American Scenery,* and possibly *United States Architecture.* When Shaw and William Dunlap met in Norfolk, Dunlap commented: "Shaw came in, just return'd from Savannah, Augusta, etc and represents the South as a paradise of riches. He says he obtained more subscribers to his work in Savannah, and that after the fire than any place in ye U.S."[84]

While in Savannah Shaw also made drawings of the great fire of 1820 and the Branch Bank of the United States, which was later engraved by William Mason and published by I. C. Kayser and Co. in 1823. This engraving was the source of the image of the bank that was reproduced in Ridgway's "Beauties of America." Because ground was not broken for the Branch Bank of the United States until April 27, 1820, and also because the engraving after Shaw's drawing differs in architectural details from later engravings and photographs of the completed bank building, it is probable that Shaw based his drawing on the architect William Jay's rendering.[85] Both English-born, Shaw and Jay were seeking their fortunes in the United States when their paths crossed briefly in Savannah. Destiny brought success to only one. The artist-inventor Shaw prospered and retired to a comfortable old age in Bordentown, New Jersey. On the other hand, Jay's architectural practice in Savannah never recovered from the difficult year of 1820, when a devastating fire and yellow fever epidemic followed the financial panic of 1819. The gifted, young architect returned to England and, after a decade of struggle, accepted an appointment in the distant colony of Mauritius, where he died prematurely in 1837.

84. Quoted in Jessie Poesch, *The Art of the Old South: . . .* (1983), p. 182. One of the subscribers to Shaw's *United States Directory* was Joseph Truchelut, the Savannah confectioner whose advertisement is reproduced in fig. 15.

85. Hanna H. Lerski, *William Jay, Itinerant English Architect, 1792–1837* (1983), pp. 152–154.

GLASSWARE

Tableware

34a +Syllabub or Jelly Glass (8). *Ca.* 1790–1800, English. Cut glass. H. 4 1/4″ (10.8 cm.). Richardson-Owens-Thomas House Collection.

34b* Wine Rinse (3). *Ca.* 1810–1820, Anglo-Irish. Cut glass. H. 4 1/4″ (10.8 cm.), diam. 5 1/4″ (13.2 cm.).

34c Wine or Champagne Glass (3). *Ca.* 1820–1840, Anglo-Irish. Glass. H. 7 1/4″ (18.4 cm.).

Early in the nineteenth century, Georgia was a state of highly diversified social strata. So much so that Daniel Mulford wrote to his sister Betsey Crane: "This state is very large. . . . In the back country, gourd shells are common for drinking cups."[86] The more affluent citizens of Savannah, however, could boast a variety of tableware requisite to highly civilized life.

Useful though they are, estate documents only give an overview of glassware. They are rarely detailed enough to shed much light on individual pieces of glassware owned by nineteenth-century Savannahians. Unlike silver, furniture, or jewelry, glass is all but never mentioned in wills. And compilers of inventories often lumped crockery and glassware together, especially when dealing with humdrum, middle-class estates. The vagueness of most notations makes a listing as general as "120 pieces of glassware" seem like a "find." The discovery of a few descriptive terms designating style and use provides welcome details about the specialized articles called for in fashionable dining. When described at all in estate documents, the only differentiation was usually "rich cut" versus "plain" or "common." An isolated reference to

Left to right: 34c, 34a, 34b, 34a, 34c

etched glass is the "1 doz flowered wine glasses" recorded in the household memorandum of William Gibbons. Water tumblers and wine glasses were the basic necessities for the dinner table. The belongings of most middle-class people contained at least a few of each. Less numerous, but substantial nonetheless, were the entries of "wash hand" or "finger" glasses, which in modern parlance are not glasses at all, but bowls.[87]

Additional forms of glassware augmented the basics at the dinner table and at large-scale afternoon or evening entertainments. Jelly, syllabub, lemonade, champagne, and cordial glasses cropped up consistently among the possessions of Savannah's wealthier citizens. For instance, William Gibbons' account book reveals that he purchased "2 glass salvers" and "2 dozen jelly glasses" from Mary Chrysties's New York shop in July 1802. His purpose was undoubtedly to use the two in combination to create a dazzling pyramid of jellies on the stacked, graduated salvers.[88]

The estate documents of Gibbons' nephew Alexander Telfair show that he owned six dozen jelly, four dozen lemonade, and two dozen champagne glasses as well as a set of glass containing fifty pieces.[89] These accoutrements of genteel pastimes dovetail with the evidence provided by Telfair's spacious house and his life as a public figure.[90] Taken all together, they suggest that he entertained as befitted a man of his station. While no narrative accounts of Telfair's parties have come to light, a notation in a family cookbook gives a sampling of the delectables that might have been served in glassware at a soirée. To complement various cakes, and dried and seasonal fruits, there were cordials: aniseed, Perfect *Amour,* cinnamon, and peach; wines: white, red, sweet red, punch red, and mead; creams: orange, lemon, and iced; and jellies: orange, quince, swinesfoot, and matrimony, which augmented the wines. "After these things," the author noted, "lemonade, sweet wines, custards of lemon, syllabubs and small cakes are handed about in profusion."[91]

86. Daniel Mulford letter to Betsey Crane, February 15, 1809 (Manuscript Collection 579, Georgia Historical Society).

87. For observations on the use of finger bowls, see Chapter One.

88. "1 Glass Pyramid & 3 doz: Glasses," inventory of Joseph Clay (1805); "2 glass pyramids" and "2 doz Jelly glasses," inventory of Joseph Habersham (1832); and "1 Stand & 22 Jelly Glasses," inventory of Henry McAlpin (1851).

89. Inventory of Alexander Telfair (1833). Although no other decedent in our survey matched Alexander Telfair in numbers of lemonade, jelly, and champagne glasses, the following inventories included one or more of those items: Delia Bryan (1827), Nicholas Bayard (1828), John Screven (1831), Joseph Habersham (1832), John Williamson (1843), and Henry McAlpin (1851).

90. For a biographical sketch of Alexander Telfair, see Feay Shellman, *The Octagon Room* (1982), pp. 9–15.

91. "Recipe Book for Puddings, etc." (Manuscript Collection 793, Georgia Historical Society). Perfect *Amour* was a cordial that was sold by confectioners. Swinesfoot jelly was clear. Jellies made from hooves of other animals, such as sheep, were amber colored. Matrimony was a frozen peach and cream dessert.

Left to right: 35a, 35b

35c

Specialized Serving Pieces

35a* Sugar Bowl with Cover. *Ca.* 1820–1830, Anglo-Irish or American (possibly Pittsburgh, Bakewell, Page, and Bakewell, 1808–1882). Cut glass. H. 8 3/16″ (20.8 cm.), diam. 5 1/8″ (13.1 cm.). Bequest of Mary Telfair, 1875.

35b* Compote. *Ca.* 1825–1830, Anglo-Irish or American (possibly Pittsburgh, Bakewell, Page, and Bakewell, 1808–1882). Cut glass. H. 4 7/8″ (12.4 cm.), diam. 7 5/16″ (18.6 cm.). Gift of Mrs. E. P. Lawton, 1961.

35c Celery Vase. *Ca.* 1825–1840, Anglo-Irish. Cut glass. H. 7 7/8″ (20 cm.), diam. 5″ (12.7 cm.). Bequest of Mary White Jackson, 1952.

Like other dining accessories, glassware reflected the owner's social station. Consequently, "rich cut" glass, a greater status symbol, soon outstripped clear flint in popularity with the American public. The sugar basin and compote in the Telfair collection beautifully exemplify the cut wares that Americans found so desirable. Both are cut in the strawberry-diamond and fan pattern brought to America by English craftsmen who settled at factories such as Bakewell, Page, and Bakewell in Pittsburgh.

Because techniques used in glassmaking—freeblowing and cutting—endured over long periods and craftsmen moved from place to place, it is really not possible to definitely assign a given piece to a particular factory without documentation. Certain formal characteristics, nevertheless, are generally associated with the manufactures of Pittsburgh. They include the knop on the stem of the sugar bowl, the general shape of the compote, and the strawberry-diamond and fan patterns of cutting.

Given the ambiguity of estate documents on the subject of glass, it is not surprising that few of the glass pieces in the Telfair collection correspond to named pieces found in our survey of Savannah estates. Although only celery vases received specific mention in our survey, Savannahians undoubtedly owned sugar basins and compotes as well.[92] Evidence from other sources tends to corroborate this assumption. For instance, a selection of fruit—including peaches, nectarines, figs, melons, and grapes—that was set down in a Telfair family cookbook would have made a decorative and delicious display for a compote.[93] Decanters, those essentials to the exchange of social amenities, as well as preserve basins, cake dishes, butter dishes, candlesticks, salts, and salvers were itemized in inventories selected for our study.

92. "2 cellary cups," inventory of Joseph Habersham (1832); "Three Celery Stands," inventory of John Williamson (1843).

93. "Recipe Book for Puddings, etc."

Appendices

Appendix I. The Gibbons and Telfair Family Genealogy

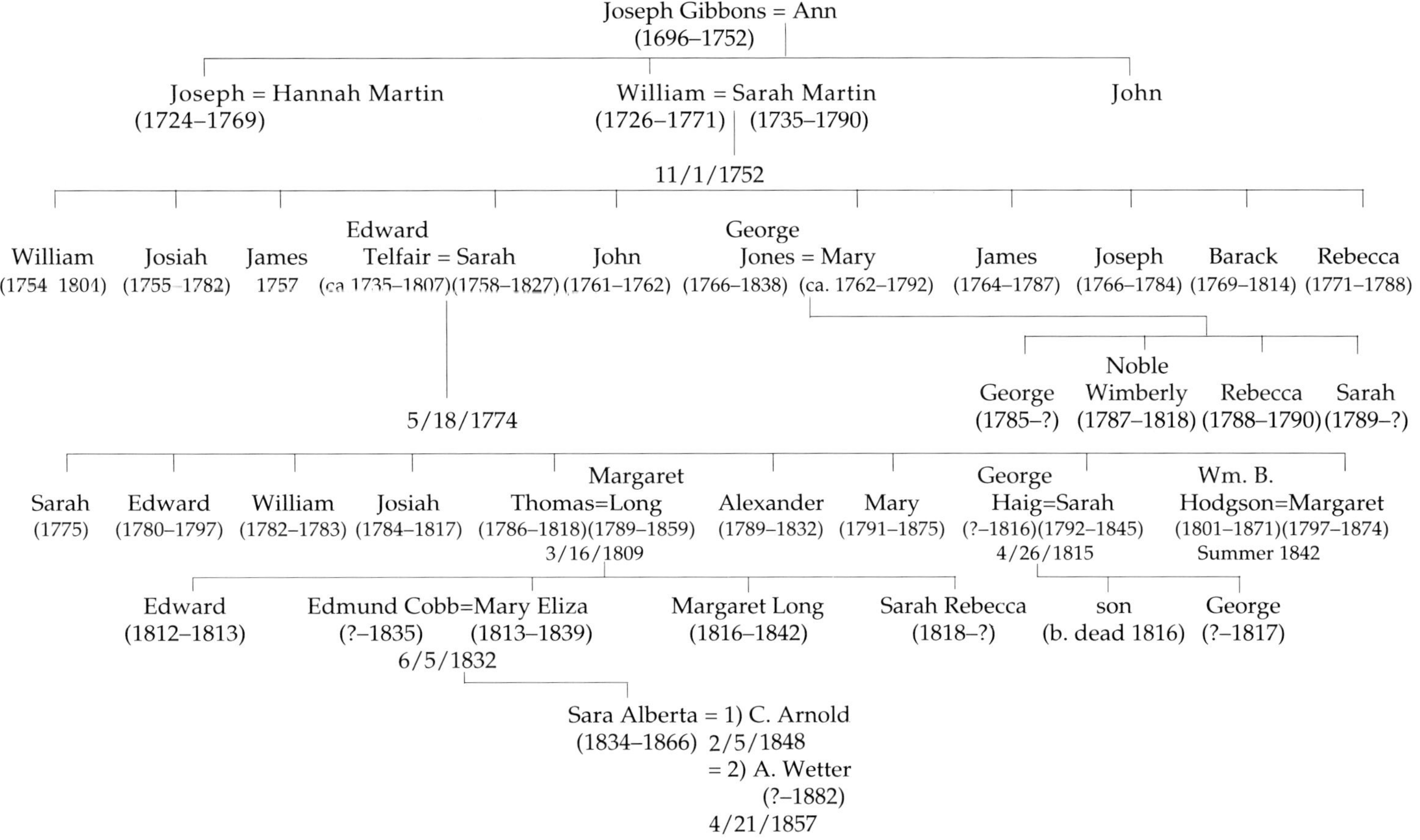

Appendix II: Architectural Designs and Commissions of William Jay (1792–1837)

1809
*Exhibited *Design for a Public Library,* Royal Academy, Somerset House, London (design now lost).

1810
*Exhibited *Design for a Boat-house,* Royal Academy, Somerset House, London (design now lost).

1812
*Exhibited *Design for a Grecian Casine,* Royal Academy, Somerset House, London (design now lost).

1815
*Exhibited *Design for a Boat-house* and a *Prospect Room,* Royal Academy, Somerset House, London (designs now lost).

1816
*Designed and built Albion Chapel, Moorgate, Shoreditch Parish, London, for the Reverend Alexander Fletcher (now destroyed).
*Designed and began construction of square-plan villa [completed 1819], Oglethorpe Square, Savannah, for Richard Richardson (now Richardson-Owens-Thomas House).

1817
*Exhibited *Sketch for Church now erecting at Savannah in America,* Royal Academy, Somerset House, London (design now lost, church never completed).

1818
*Designed and built Savannah Theater (now greatly altered).
*Designed and built square-plan villa, Orleans Square, Savannah, for Archibald Stobo Bulloch (now destroyed).

*Administered contract for building Custom House and Warehouses, Savannah (now destroyed, design lost).
*Designed and built square-plan villa, West Broad Street (now Martin Luther King Boulevard), Savannah, for William Scarbrough.
*Designed and built square-plan villa, St. James (now Telfair) Square, Savannah, for Alexander Telfair (now greatly altered except for selected rooms).
*Designed and built Savannah Free School (now destroyed, design lost).
*Designed house for Robert Habersham of Savannah (design lost).
*Designed and built marine villa, Sullivan's Island, near Charleston, South Carolina (now destroyed, design lost).

1819
*Designed and built pavilion and ballroom, Johnson Square, Savannah, for President James Monroe's visit (now destroyed, design lost).
*Designed and possibly built house for Hazen Kimbell of Savannah (design lost).

1820
*Appointed architect of State Board of Public Works, Columbia, South Carolina; held position less than one year.
*Exhibited at City Hall, Charleston, a model of a series of buildings designed for the Public Square (designs now lost).
*Designed and constructed the Branch Bank of the United States, Savannah (now destroyed).
*Designed and constructed house, Meeting Street, Charleston, for William Mason Smith.

1824
*Designed and built row of houses, Columbia Place, Cheltenham, Gloucestershire, for Joseph Pitt, developer of Pittville section of Cheltenham.

1825
*Designed and built Watermoor House, square-plan villa, near Cirencester, Gloucestershire, for Joseph Randolph Mullings.

1826
*Designed and built a row of houses, Pittville Parade, Evesham Road, Cheltenham, Gloucestershire.

1829
Enlarged congregational church, Henley on Thames, Oxon, for the Reverend Robert Bolton.

1836
*Appointed Assistant Chief Architect and Inspector of Works for Colony of Mauritius; held position at his death in 1837.
*Designed Congregational Chapel, Port Louis, Mauritius (design altered).

Appendix III: Bills of Fare

Accounts of six dinners have been pared down to lists of dishes in order to give an overview of actual bills of fare. The writers did not include the same kinds of detail so the lists cannot be exactly parallel. Unfortunately it was impossible to include descriptive comments, such as "a ham, which Mr. C. informed us cost three times as much as American hams,"[1] "a very unseemly piece of cheese,"[2] and "a pyramid of Ice, rivalling those of Egypt."[3]

Dinner given by:	Dr. Kolloch (a clergy man)	Mr. C——.	Mr. Taylor (Governor of S.C.)	Mr. Clinton (Governor of N.Y.)	Mrs. Skirving (an Englishwoman)	Mr. Alston
Where:	Savannah	Savannah	Columbia, S.C.	Albany, N.Y.	Jacksonburgh, S.C.	Rice Plantation, coastal S.C
Date:	April 5, 1822	April 1818	February 1828	September 1827	March 1828	October 18, 1832
Time:	—	4:00 P.M.	—	—	2:00 P.M.	
Recorded by:	J. Evarts[4]	Mrs. Hillhouse[5]	Mrs. Hall[6]	Mrs. Hall[7]	Mrs. Hall[8]	John B. Grimball[9]
First Course:	dumb fish (cod) Southern bacon ducks oysters (2 ways) bread onions beets boiled rice Irish potatoes (2 ways)	fish ham chicken pie oysters shrimp crab lettuce dressed as salad	fish ham roast ducks corned beef turkeys—roasted and boiled chickens beet root rice Irish potatoes sweet potatoes cabbage	ham roast ducks roast beef boiled mutton beans turnips potatoes	boiled turkey roast chicken asparagus peas potatoes	turtle soup leg of boiled mutton turtle steaks and fins(2) pie of macaroni small dish of oysters (2) boiled ham haunch of venison roast turkey
Second Course:[10]	cherry pie cranberry pie quince, orange, and other preserves salad cheese butter pineapple cream	apple dumplings cheese puffs in great variety finger glasses	pies (8) 6 dishes of glasses of syllabub 6 dishes of glasses of jelly floating islands ginger other preserves	bread pudding biscuits cheese pyramid of ice sweetmeats (2) peaches plums melons (2) grapes (2)	rice custard sweetmeats	bread pudding jelly high glass dish of ice cream a pie Madeira sherry champagne
Dessert:	oranges plantains raisins walnuts cordials wine	olives wines				bananas oranges apples Hermitage Madeira cordials

1. Marion Alexander Boggs, *The Alexander Letters, 1787–1900* (1980), p. 50.
2. Mrs. Basil Hall, *The Aristocratic Journey*, . . . (1931), p. 66.
3. *Ibid.*
4. Jeremiah Evarts, Diary, 1822.
5. Boggs, p. 50.
6. Mrs. Basil Hall, pp. 208–209.
7. *Ibid.*, p.66.
8. *Ibid.*, p. 221.
9. Quoted in Sam Bowers Hilliard, *Hog Meat and Hoecake*: . . . (1972), p. 54.
10. At some tables the second and dessert courses were combined.

Selected Bibliography

BOOKS AND ARTICLES

Albany Institute of History and Art. *New York Furniture Before 1840 in the Collection of the Albany Institute of History and Art.* Albany, N.Y., 1962.

Alcott, William A. *The Young Housekeeper or Thoughts on Food and Cookery.* Boston: George W. Light, 1842.

Andrews, William L., intro. *Six Women's Slave Narratives.* New York–Oxford: Oxford University Press, 1988.

Armstrong, John. *The Young Woman's Guide to Virtue, Economy, and Happiness.* Newcastle upon Tyne: Mackenzie and Dent, [1817]

Atlanta Historical Society. *Neat Pieces: The Plain-style Furniture of 19th Century Georgia.* Atlanta, 1983.

The Baltimore Museum of Art. *Eighteenth and Nineteenth Century Maryland Silver in the Collection of the Baltimore Museum of Art.* Baltimore, 1975.

Bancroft, Joseph. *Census of the City of Savannah.* Savannah: Edward J. Purse, Printer, 1848.

Barnum, H. L. *Family Receipts or Practical Guide for the Husbandman and Housewife.* Cincinnati: A. B. Roff, 1831.

Beeton, Mrs. Isabella. *The Book of Household Management.* London: S. O. Beeton, 1861.

Belden, Louise Conway. *The Festive Tradition: Table Decoration and Desserts in America, 1650–1900.* New York–London: W. W. Norton & Co., 1983.

———. *Marks of American Silversmiths in the Ineson-Bissell Collection.* Charlottesville: Published for the Henry Francis du Pont Winterthur Museum by the University Press of Virginia, 1980.

Bell, Malcolm, Jr. *Major Butler's Legacy: Five Generations of a*

Slaveholding Family. Athens–London: University of Georgia Press, 1987.

Benes, Peter, ed. *Food Ways in the Northeast.* Boston: Boston University, 1984.

Bernhard Karl, Duke of Saxe-Weimar Eisenach. *Travels Through North America During the Years 1825–1826.* Philadelphia: Carey, Lea, and Carey, 1828.

Betts, Edwin M., ed. *Thomas Jefferson's Garden Book, 1766–1824.* Philadelphia: American Philosophical Society, 1944.

Blocker, Jack S., Jr. *American Temperance Movements: Cycles of Reform.* Boston: Twayne Publishers, 1989.

Boggs, Marion Alexander. *The Alexander Letters, 1787–1900.* Athens: University of Georgia Press, 1980.

Bonner, James C. *A History of Georgia Agriculture, 1732–1860* Athens: University of Georgia Press, 1964.

Boorstin, Daniel J. *The Americans: The National Experience.* New York: Random House, 1965.

Bordley, John Beale. *Essays and Notes on Husbandry and Rural Affairs.* Philadelphia: Thomas Dobson, 1801.

Bradbury, Frederick. *History of Old Sheffield Plate.* London: Macmillan & Co., Ltd., 1912.

Breeden, James O. *Advice Among Masters: The Ideal in Slave Management in the Old South.* Westport, Conn.: Greenwood Press, 1980.

Bremer, Fredrika. *The Homes of the New World: Impressions of America.* Trans. by Mary Howitt. London: Arthur Hall, Virtue, and Co., 1853.

Brewer, Priscilla J. "'We Have Got a Very Good Cooking Stove,'—Advertising, Design, and Consumer Response to the Cookstove, 1815–1880." *Winterthur Portfolio* 25, pt. 1 (Spring 1990): 35–54.

Brix, Maurice. *List of Philadelphia Silversmiths and Allied Artificers from 1682–1850.* Philadelphia: privately printed, 1920.

Brown, Michael Kevin. "Duncan Phyfe." Master's thesis, University of Delaware, 1978.

Brown, Robert. "Six Philadelphia Cabinetmakers: Johnathan Gostelowe, David Evans, Ephraim Haines, Henry Connelly, John Aitken, Joseph Barry." Student paper, University of Delaware, 1960.

Buckingham, James Silk. *The Slave States of America.* Repr. of 1842 ed. New York: Negro University Press, 1968.

Burke, Emily P. *Reminiscences of Georgia.* Oberlin: James M. Fitch, 1850.

Burton, E. Milby. *South Carolina Silversmiths, 1690–1860.* Charleston: The Charleston Museum, 1942.

Busby, Charles A. *A Collection of Designs for Modern Embellishments Suitable to Parlours, Dining and Drawing Rooms, Folding Doors, Chimney Pieces, Varandas, Friezes, Etc.* London: J. Taylor, 1810.

Byrne, William A. "The Burden and the Heat of the Day: Slavery and Servitude in Savannah, 1733–1865." Ph.D. diss., Florida State University, 1979.

Camehl, Ada Walker. *The Blue-China Book: Early American Scenes and History Pictured in the Pottery of the Time.* New York: Tudor Publishing Co., 1946.

Candler, Myrtie Long. "Reminiscences of Life in Georgia During the 1850's and 60's." *Georgia Historical Quarterly*: 33, pt. 2 (June 1949), 110–123; 33, pt. 3 (September 1949), 218–227; 33, pt. 4 (December 1949), 303–313; and 34, pt. 1 (March 1950), 10–18.

Carolina Art Association. *Selections From the Collection of the Carolina Art Association.* Charleston, 1977.

Carson, Barbara G. *Ambitious Appetites, Dining Behavior, and Patterns of Consumption in Federal Washington.* Washington, D.C.: American Institute of Architects Press, 1990.

Carson, Jane. *Colonial Virginia Cookery.* Williamsburg: The Colonial Williamsburg Foundation, 1968.

Catalano, Kathleen Matilda. "Cabinetmaking in Philadelphia, 1820–1840." Master's thesis, University of Delaware, 1972.

Clinton, Catherine. *The Plantation Mistress: Woman's World in the Old South.* New York: Pantheon Books, 1982.

Cobbett, William. *A Year's Residence in the United States of America.* London: Sherwood, Neely, and Jones, 1818.

Coleman, Kenneth, ed. *A History of Georgia.* Athens: The University of Georgia Press, 1977.

Cooke, Edward S., Jr. "Domestic Space in the Federal-Period Inventories of Salem Merchants." *Essex Institute Historical Collections* 16, pt. 4 (October 1980): 248–264.

Cooper, Wendy A. *In Praise of America.* New York: Alfred A. Knopf, 1980.

Cosnett, Thomas. *The Footman's Directory and Butler's Remembrancer.* London: J. Hatchard and Son, 1823.

Coulter, E. Merton. "A Century of a Georgia Plantation." *Agricultural History* 3, pt. 4 (October 1929): 147–159.

Coysh, A. W. *Blue-printed Earthenware, 1800–1850.* Tokyo–Rutland: Charles E. Tuttle Co., Inc., 1972.

Cummings, Richard O. *The American and His Food.* Facsimile of the 1940 ed. New York: Arno Press, 1970.

———. *The American Ice Harvests: A Historical Study in Technology, 1800–1918.* Berkeley: University of California Press, 1949.

Cunningham, Noble E., Jr., ed. "The Diary of Frances Few, 1808–1809." *Journal of Southern History* 21, pt. 3 (August 1963): 345–361.

Cutten, George Barton. *The Silversmiths of Georgia, Together With Watchmakers and Jewelers, 1733 to 1850.* Savannah: The Pigeonhole Press, 1958.

The Darling Foundation of New York State. *New York State Silversmiths.* New York, 1964.

Davis, Harold E. *The Fledgling Province: Social and Cultural Life in Colonial Georgia, 1733–1776.* Chapel Hill: The University of North Carolina Press, 1976.

Davis, John. *Travels of Four Years and a Half in the United States of America During 1798, 1799, 1800, 1801, and 1802.* Repr. of 1803 ed. New York: Henry Holt & Co., 1909. With introduction by A. J. Morrison.

Davis, Matthew L. *Memoirs of Aaron Burr; With Miscellaneous Selections From His Correspondence.* New York: Harper and Brothers, 1837.

Deak, Gloria Gilda. *Picturing America, 1497–1899: Prints, Maps, and Drawings Bearing on the New World Discoveries and on the Development of the Territory That Is Now the United States.* Princeton: Princeton University Press, 1988.

The Domestic's Companion. New York: Edward W. Martin, 1834.

Dow, George Francis. "Trade Cards." *Old-Time New England: The Bulletin of the Society for the Preservation of New England Antiquities* 26, pt. 4 (April 1936): 114–135; and 27, pt. 1 (July 1936): 10–22.

Downs, Joseph, and Ruth Ralston. *A Loan Exhibition of New York State Furniture.* New York: The Metropolitan Museum of Art, 1934.

Duncan, John M. *Travels Through Part of the United States and Canada in 1818 and 1819.* 2 vols. Glasgow: Hurst, Robinson, & Co., 1823.

Easterby, J. H., ed. *The South Carolina Rice Plantation as Revealed in the Papers of Robert F. W. Allston.* Chicago: University of Chicago Press, 1945.

Eaton, Mary. *The Cook and Housekeeper's Complete and Universal Dictionary.* Bungay: I. and R. Childs, 1822.

Evans, Richard Xavier, contributor. "Letters From Robert Mills." *The South Carolina Historical and Genealogical Magazine* 39, pt. 3 (July 1938): 103–124.

Fales, Martha Gandy. *Early American Silver.* New York: E. P. Dutton and Co., Inc., 1970.

———. *Joseph Richardson and Family, Philadelphia Silversmiths.* Middletown: Wesleyan University Press, 1974.

Farnham, Katherine Gross, and Callie Huger Efird. "Early Silversmiths and the Silver Trade in Georgia." *Antiques* 99, pt. 3 (March 1971): 380–385.

[Farrar, Eliza Ware (Rotch)]. *The Young Lady's Friend by a Lady.* Boston: American Stationers' Company, 1837.

Federal Writer's Project. *Georgia: A Guide to Its Towns and Countryside.* Repr. of 1940 ed. St. Clair Shores, Mich.: Somerset Publishers, 1973.

The Female Instructor or Young Woman's Companion. Liverpool: Nuttall, Fisher, and Dixon, [1811].

Gardiner, Ann Gibbons. *Mrs. Gardiner's Receipts From 1763.* Hallowell: White, Horn, & Co., 1938.

Garrett, Elisabeth Donaghy. "The American Home, Part IV: The Dining Room." *Antiques* 126, pt. 4 (October 1984): 910–922.

———. "The American Home, Part VI: The Quest for Comfort: Housekeeping Practices and Living Arrangements the Year Round." *Antiques* 128, pt. 6 (December 1985): 1210–1223.

———. *At Home: The American Family, 1750–1870.* New York: Harry N. Abrams, Inc., Publishers, 1990.

Garvan, Beatrice B. *Federal Philadelphia 1785–1825: The Athens of the Western World.* Philadelphia: Philadelphia Museum of Art, 1987.

Georgia Museum of Art. *Georgia's Legacy: History Charted Through the Arts.* Athens: University of Georgia Press, 1985.

Gilman, Caroline H. *Recollections of a Southern Matron.* Charleston: Walker, Richards and Co., 1852.

Goldsborough, Jennifer Faulds. *Silver in Maryland.* Baltimore: Museum and Library of Maryland History, Maryland Historical Society, 1983.

Gottesman, Rita Susswein. *The Arts and Crafts in New York, 1800–1804.* New York: New-York Historical Society, 1965.

Green, Robert Alan. *Marks of American Silversmiths.* Harrison, N.J.: R. A. Green, 1977.

———. "Silversmiths of Georgia 1733–1860." *Silver* 10, pt. 4 (July–August 1977): 10–13.

Gross, Katharine Wood. "The Sources of Furniture Sold in Savannah, 1789–1815." Master's thesis, University of Delaware, 1967.

Hall, Basil. *Forty Etchings, From Sketches Made With the Camera Lucida, in North America, in 1827 and 1828.* 3 vols. Edinburgh: Cadell & Co., 1829.

Hall, Mrs. Basil. *The Aristocratic Journey, Being the Outspoken Letters of Mrs. Basil Hall, Written During a Fourteen Months' Sojourn in America 1827–1828.* Ed. by Una Pope-Hennessy. New York: G. P. Putnam's Sons, 1931.

Hall, Elizabeth M. *Practical American Cookery and Domestic Economy.* New York: Miller, Orton, and Mulligan, 1856.

Hamilton, Thomas. *Men and Manners in America.* 2 vols. London: T. Cadell, 1833.

Hardee, Charles Seton Henry. *Reminiscences and Recollections of Old Savannah.* [Savannah]: Privately printed, n.d.

Harriott, John. *Struggles Through Life, Exemplified in the Various Travels and Adventures in Europe, Asia, Africa, and America, of Lt. John Harriott, Now Resident Magistrate of the Thames Police.* Philadelphia: John Humphreys, 1809.

Harris, J. William. *Plain Folk and Gentry in a Slave Society—White Liberty and Black Slavery in Augusta's Hinterlands.* Middletown, Conn.: Wesleyan University Press, 1985.

Hartridge, Walter C., Jr., ed. *The Letters of Don Juan McQueen to His Family, Written From Spanish East Florida, 1791–1807.* Columbia, S.C.: Bostick and Thornley, 1943.

———. *The Letters of Robert Mackay to His Wife, Written From Ports in America and England, 1795–1816.* Athens: The University of Georgia Press, under the auspices of the Georgia Society of the Colonial Dames of America, 1949.

Heckscher, Morrison H. "The Organization and Practice of Philadelphia Cabinetmaking Establishments, 1790–1820." Master's thesis, University of Delaware, 1964.

Hilliard, Sam Bowers. *Hog Meat and Hoecake: Food Supply in the Old South, 1840–1860.* Carbondale: Southern Illinois University Press, 1972.

Hodgson, Adam. *Letters From North America, Written During a Tour in the United States and Canada.* London: Hurst, Robinson, and Co., 1824.

Holgate, David. *New Hall and Its Imitators.* London: Faber & Faber, 1971.

Holmes, Francis S. *The Southern Farmer and Market Gardener.* Charleston: William R. Babcock, and McCarter & Co., 1852.

Holmes, James. *"Dr. Bullie's" Notes: Reminiscences of Early Georgia and of Philadelphia and New Haven in the 1800s.* Ed. by Delma Eugene Presley. Atlanta: Cherokee Publishing Company, 1976.

Hooker, Richard J. *Food and Drink in America, A History.* New York: The Bobbs-Merrill Company, Inc., 1981.

Hooker, Richard J., ed. *A Colonial Plantation Cookbook: The Receipt Book of Harriott Pinckney Horry, 1770.* Columbia: University of South Carolina Press, 1984.

Howard, David S. *New York and the China Trade.* New York: The New-York Historical Society, 1984.

Hughes, G. Bernard. *Antique Sheffield Plate.* London: B. T. Batsford Ltd., 1970.

Innes, Lowell. *Pittsburgh Glass, 1797–1891—A History and Guide for Collectors.* Boston: Houghton Mifflin Co., 1976.

Johnson, Guion Griffis. *A Social History of the Sea Islands, With Special Reference to St. Helena Island, South Carolina.* Repr. of 1930 Chapel Hill ed. New York: Negro Universities Press, 1969.

Jones, Katherine M. *The Plantation South.* Indianapolis–New York: Bobbs-Merrill Company, Inc., 1957.

Jordan, James C., III. "The Neoclassical Dining Room in Charleston." *Journal of Early Southern Decorative Arts* 14, pt. 2 (November 1988): 1–25.

Kemble, Frances Anne. *Journal of a Residence on a Georgian Plantation in 1838–1839.* Ed. by John A. Scott. New York: Alfred A. Knopf, 1961.

Kennedy, Roger G. *Architecture, Men, Women, and Money in America, 1600–1860.* New York: Random House, 1985.

Killion, Ronald G., and Charles Waller. *Slavery Time When I Was Chillun Down on Marster's Plantation: Interviews With Georgia Slaves.* Savannah: The Beehive Press, 1973.

Kitchiner, William. *The Cook's Oracle: Containing Receipts for Plain Cookery on the Most Economical Plan for Private Families.* Boston: Munroe and Francis, 1822.

Klamkin, Marian. *American Patriotic and Political China.* New York: Charles Scribner's Sons, 1973.

A Lady. *The Home Book; or, Young Housekeeper's Assistant.* London: Smith, Elder, and Co., 1829.

Landauer, Bella C. *Early American Trade Cards From the Collection of Bella C. Landauer.* New York: William Edwin Rudge, 1927. With critical notes by Adele Jenny.

Lane, Mills B., ed. *The Rambler in Georgia.* Savannah: The Beehive Press, 1973.

Larsen, Ellouise Baker. *American Historical Views on Staffordshire China.* New York: Doubleday, Doran and Company, Inc., 1939.

Lerski, Hanna H. *William Jay, Itinerant English Architect, 1792–1837.* Lanham, Md.: University Press of America, Inc., 1983.

Leslie, Eliza. *The House Book: or, a Manual of Domestic Economy.* Philadelphia: Carey and Hart, 1841.

Longstreet, Augustus B. *Georgia Scenes, Characters, Incidents &c. in the First Half Century of the Republic.* Repr. of the 1835 Augusta ed. Savannah: The Beehive Press, 1975.

Lyell, Sir Charles. *A Second Visit to the United States of North America.* 2 vols. London: John Murray, 1849.

Martineau, Harriet. *Society in America.* New York: Saunders and Otley, 1837.

McAllister, Ward. *Society as I Have Found It.* Repr. of the 1890 New York ed. New York: Arno Press, 1975.

McClelland, Nancy. *Duncan Phyfe and the English Regency, 1795–1830.* Repr. of the 1939 New York ed. New York: Dover Publications, Inc., 1980.

McClinton, Katharine Morrison. *Collecting American Nineteenth Century Silver.* New York: Charles Scribner's Sons, 1968.

McDonough, James V. "William Jay, Regency Architect in Georgia and South Carolina." Ph.D. diss., Princeton University, 1950.

The Metropolitan Museum of Art. *Nineteenth-Century America: Furniture and Other Decorative Arts.* New York, 1970.

Miller, V. Isabelle. *Silver by New York Makers, Late 17th Century to 1900.* New York: The Museum of the City of New York, 1937.

Montgomery, Charles F. *American Furniture: The Federal Period 1788–1825.* Repr. of 1966 ed. New York: Bonanza Books, 1978.

Mudge, Jean McClure. *Chinese Export Porcelain for the American Trade 1785–1835.* Newark: University of Delaware Press, 1981.

The Museum of Fine Arts, Houston. *Southern Silver—An Exhibition of Silver Made in the South Prior to 1860.* Houston, 1968.

Myers, Robert M., ed. *The Children of Pride: A True Story of Georgia and the Civil War.* New Haven: Yale University Press, 1972.

Neilson, Peter. *Recollections of a Six-years Residence in the United States of America.* Edinburgh: William Tate, 1830.

The Newark Museum. *Classical America 1815–1845.* Newark, N.J., 1963.

Nissenbaum, Stephen. *Sex, Diet, and Debility in Jacksonian America—Sylvester Graham and Health Reform.* Westport, Conn.: Greenwood Press, 1980.

Nutting, Wallace. *Furniture Treasury (Mostly of American Origin) All Periods of American Furniture With Some Foreign Examples in America.* Framingham, Mass.: Old America Co., 1928–1933.

Nylander, Jane C. "Henry Sargent's *Dinner Party* and *Tea Party.*" *Antiques* 21, pt. 5 (May 1982): 1172–1183.

Okie, Harold Pitcher. *Old Silver and Old Sheffield Plate: A History of the Silversmith's Art in Great Britain and Ireland.* Garden City, N.Y.: Doubleday, Doran, 1936.

Olmsted, Frederick Law. *The Cotton Kingdom: A Traveller's Observations on Cotton and Slavery in the American Slave States.* New York: Alfred A. Knopf, 1953.

Otto, John S. *Cannon's Point Plantation, 1794–1860: Living Conditions and Status Patterns in the Old South.* Orlando, Fla.: Academic Press, Inc., 1984.

Parkes, Frances B. *Domestic Duties.* New York: J. and J. Harper, 1829.

Parloa, Maria. *Miss Parloa's Kitchen Companion.* Boston: Estes and Lauriat, 1887.

Pease, Jane H. "A Note on Patterns of Conspicuous Consumption Among Seaboard Planters, 1820–1860." *Journal of Southern History* 35, pt. 3 (August 1969): 381–393.

Pleasants, J. Hall, and Howard Sill. *Maryland Silversmiths, 1715–1830.* Baltimore: Lord Baltimore Press, 1930.

Poesch, Jessie J. *The Art of the Old South: Painting, Sculpture, Architecture and the Products of Craftsmen, 1560–1860.* New York: Alfred A. Knopf, 1983.

Power, Tyrone. *Impressions of America; During the Years 1833, 1834, and 1835.* Philadelphia: Carey, Lea and Blanchard, 1836.

Rainwater, Dorothy T. *American Silver Manufacturers.* Hanover: Everybody's Press, 1966.

Randolph, Mary. *The Virginia House-wife.* Columbia: University of South Carolina Press, 1984. With historical notes and commentaries by Karen Hess.

Rawick, George P., ed. *The American Slave: A Composite Autobiography.* 19 vols. Supplement series 1, 12 vols.; Supplement Series 2, 10 vols., repr. of 1941 ed. Westport, Conn.: Greenwood Press, 1972–1979.

Roberts, Robert. *The House Servant's Directory.* Facsimile of the 1827 Boston ed. Waltham, Mass.: The Gore Place Society, 1977.

Root, Waverly, and Richard de Rochemont. *Eating in America: A History.* New York: William Morrow & Co., Inc., 1976.

[Rundell, Mrs. Maria Eliza]. *A New System of Domestic Cookery, Formed Upon Principles of Economy, and Adapted to the Use of Private Families. By a Lady.* New York, 1817.

Rutledge, Anna Wells. "After the Cloth Was Removed." *Winterthur Portfolio IV.* Charlottesville: University Press of Virginia, 1968.

[Rutledge, Sarah]. *The Carolina Housewife.* Facsimile of the 1847 Charleston ed., introduction and preliminary checklist of South Carolina cookbooks published before 1935 by Anna Wells Rutledge. Columbia: University of South Carolina Press, 1979.

Salley, A. S., ed. "The Journal of General Peter Horry." *The South Carolina Historical and Genealogical Magazine:* 38, pt. 2 (April 1937): 49–53; 38, pt. 3 (July 1937): 81–86; 38, pt. 4 (October 1937): 116–119; 39, pt. 1 (January 1938): 46–49; 39, pt. 2 (April 1938): 96–99; 39, pt. 3 (July 1938): 125–128; 39, pt. 4 (October 1938): 157–159; 40, pt. 1 (January 1939): 11–14; 40, pt. 2 (April 1939): 49–51; 40, pt. 3 (July 1939): 91–96; 40, pt. 3 (July 1939): 91–96; 40, pt. 4 (October 1939): 142–144.

Samuel Kirk and Son, Inc. *Kirk Silver in United States Museums.* Baltimore, 1967.

Samuel Kirk and Son Museum of Baltimore, Maryland. *Samuel Kirk and Son: American Silver Craftsmen Since 1815.* n.d.

Savannah Unit, Georgia Writer's Project, Work Project Administration. *Drums and Shadows: Survival Studies Among the Georgia Coastal Negroes.* Athens: University of Georgia Press, 1987.

Schiffer, Herbert, Peter Schiffer, and Nancy Schiffer. *Chinese Export Porcelain: Standard Patterns and Forms, 1780–1880.* Exton, Pa.: Schiffer Publishing Ltd., 1975.

Shaw, Joshua. *United States Directory for the Use of Travellers and Merchants.* Philadelphia: James Maxwell, [1822].

Shellman, Feay. *The Octagon Room.* Savannah: Telfair Academy of Arts and Sciences, Inc., 1982.

Shryock, Richard H., ed. *Letters of Richard D. Arnold, M.D., 1808–1876, Mayor of Savannah, Georgia, First Secretary of the American Medical Association.* Durham, N.C.: The Seeman Press, 1929.

Sibbald, George. *Notes and Observations, on the Pinelands of Georgia, Shewing the Advantages They Possess, Particularly in the Culture of Cotton, Addressed to Persons Emigrating, and Those Disposed to Encourage Migration to This State.* Augusta, Ga.: William J. Bunce, 1801.

Simmons, Amelia. *The First American Cookbook: A Facsimile of "American Cookery," 1796.* New York: Dover Publications, Inc., 1984. With essay by Mary Tolford Wilson.

Simon, Andre L. *A Concise Encyclopedia of Gastronomy.* New York: Harcourt, Brace, and Co., 1952.

Singleton, Theresa A., ed. *The Archaeology of Slavery and Plantation Life.* Orlando, Fla.: Academic Press, Inc., 1985.

Smith, Jane Webb. *Georgia's Legacy: History Charted Through the Arts.* Athens: Georgia Museum of Art, 1985.

Smith, Julia Floyd. *Slavery and Rice Culture in Low Country Georgia, 1750–1860.* Knoxville: The University of Tennessee Press, 1985.

Society of Cabinet Makers, London. *The London Cabinet Makers' Book of Prices, for the Most Improved Extensible Dining Tables.* London, 1815.

Southmayd, Bradbury. "Three Part Dining Tables." *The Antiquarian* 4, pt. 3 (April 1925): 10–12.

Sprackling, Helen. *Customs of the Table Top: How New England Housewives Set Out Their Tables.* Sturbridge, Mass.: Old Sturbridge Village, 1958.

Stauffer, David McNeely. *American Engravers upon Copper and Steel.* Repr. of the 1907 ed. New York: Burt Franklin, n.d.

Stoneman, Vernon C. *John and Thomas Seymour, Cabinetmakers in Boston, 1794–1816.* Boston: Special Publications, 1959.

———. *A Supplement to John and Thomas Seymour, Cabinetmakers in Boston, 1794–1816.* Boston: Special Publications, 1965.

Stuart, James. *Three Years in North America.* 2 vols. New York: J. and J. Harper, 1833.

Stuart, Sheila. "The Progress of the Dining Table." *The Antique Dealer's and Collector's Guide* 20, pt. 10 (May 1966): 56–57.

Sutcliff, Robert. *Travels in Some Parts of North America in the Years 1804, 1805, 1806.* New York: W. Alexander, 1815.

Taylor, Mrs. *Practical Hints to Young Females.* Boston: Wells and Lilly, 1816.

Thackeray, William Makepeace. *A Collection of Letters of Thackeray, 1847–1855.* New York: Charles Scribner's Sons, 1887.

Tracy, Berry B. *Federal Furniture and Decorative Arts at Boscobel.* New York: Harry N. Abrams, Inc., Publishers, 1981.

Trollope, Mrs. *Domestic Manners of the Americans.* London: Whittaker, Treacher, and Co., 1832.

Tyrrell, Ian. "Drink and Temperance in the Antebellum South: An Overview and Interpretation." *Journal of Southern History* 48, pt. 4 (November 1982): 485–510.

Universal Receipt Book or Complete Family Director. New York: A Society of Gentlemen of New York, 1814.

Wade, Richard C. *Slavery in the Cities: The South, 1820–1860.* New York: Oxford University Press, 1964.

Walker, Thomas. *The Art of Dining; and the Art of Attaining High Health.* Philadelphia: E. L. Carey and A. Hart, 1837.

Ware, William Rotch. *The Georgian Period: Being Photographs and Measured Drawings of Colonial Work With Text.* New York: U.P.C. Book Company, Inc., 1923.

Waring, Joseph Frederick. *Cerveau's Savannah.* Savannah: Georgia Historical Society, 1973.

Waxman, Lorraine. "French Influence on American Decorative Arts of the Early 19th Century; The Work of Charles-Honore Lannuier." Master's thesis, University of Delaware, 1958.

Webster, Thomas. *An Encyclopedia of Domestic Economy.* New York: Harper & Brothers, 1845.

Wenham, Edward. *Domestic Silver of Great Britain and Ireland.* New York: Oxford University Press, 1931.

White, William N. *Gardening for the South; or, How to Grow Vegetables and Fruits.* New York: Orange Judd Co., 1868.

Whitehill, Jane. *Food, Drink, and Recipes of Early New England.* Sturbridge, Mass.: Old Sturbridge Village, 1963.

Williams, James. *The Footman's Guide.* London: Dean and Munday, n.d.

Williams, James A. "Savannah Silver and Silversmiths." *Antiques* 91, pt. 3 (March 1967): 347–349.

Willich, A. F. M. *Lectures on Diet and Regimen.* Boston: Manning and [Loring], 1800.

———. *The Domestic Encyclopedia; or, The Dictionary of Facts, and Useful Knowledge.* Philadelphia: William Young Birch and Abraham Small, 1803.

Wyatt-Brown, Bertram. *Southern Honor: Ethics and Behavior in the Old South.* New York–Oxford: Oxford University Press, 1982.

Wyler, Seymour B. *The Book of Old Silver—English, American, Foreign.* New York: Crown Publishers, 1937.

The Young Woman's Companion and Instructor. Manchester: J. Aston, 1806.

MANUSCRIPTS AND MISCELLANEOUS

Appling, Wills and Inventories, 1816 Columbia County [Georgia] Courthouse.

Evarts, Jeremiah, Diary, 1822. Manuscript Collection 240, Georgia Historical Society.

Few Family, Papers, 1808–1844. Georgia Department of Archives and History.

Floyd, Charles Rinaldo, Diary, 1816–1845. Manuscript Collection 257, Georgia Historical Society.

Fox, George, The American Journals, 1831–1868. Joseph Downs Manuscript and Microfilm Collection, Henry Francis du Pont Winterthur Museum Library.

Gillow and Company Designs. Department of Prints and Drawings, Victoria and Albert Museum.

Jones, Charles Colcock, Jr., letter, Augusta, Ga., to Ruth Berrien Jones, May 11, 1888. Manuscript Collection 1349, Georgia Historical Society.

Meldrim Family, Papers, 1809–1973. Manuscript Collection 1288, Georgia Historical Society.

Mulford, Daniel, Papers, 1803–1812. Manuscript Collection 579, Georgia Historical Society.

Savannah, Wills, Inventories, and Deeds, 1800–1854. Chatham County Courthouse. All wills, inventories, and deeds cited in this study are located at the Chatham County Courthouse unless otherwise noted.

Telfair Family, Papers, 1751–1875. Manuscript Collection 793, Georgia Historical Society.

Waring Family, Papers, 1832–1849. Manuscript Collection 1275, Georgia Historical Society.

Washington, D.C., Records of the U.S. Customs Service. National Archives.

White, Anna Mathews, Papers, 1828–1832. Manuscript Collection 857, Georgia Historical Society.

Nostrums for Fashionable Entertainments
Dining in Georgia, 1800–1850

was composed by
Graphic Composition, Inc., Athens, Georgia,
and printed by
Schneidereith & Sons, Inc., Baltimore, Maryland.